All The Stars At My Party:
Celebrity Encounters in Hollywood

Jackie Frame

All The Stars At My Party:
Celebrity Encounters in Hollywood

Jackie Frame

Academica Press
Washington - London

Library of Congress Cataloging-in-Publication Data
Names: Frame, Jackie, author.
Title: All the stars at my party : celebrity encounters in Hollywood / Jackie Frame.
Other titles: Celebrity encounters in Hollywood
Description: Washington : Academica Press, [2019]
Identifiers: LCCN 2019014377| ISBN 9781680534979 (hardback : alk. paper) |
ISBN 9781680531541 (pbk. : alk. paper)
Subjects: LCSH: Los Angeles (Calif.)--Social life and customs--20th century--Anecdotes. | Hollywood (Los Angeles, Calif.)--Social life and customs--20th century--Anecdotes. | Frame, Jackie--Anecdotes. | Frame, Jackie--Friends and associates--Anecdotes. | Hollywood (Los Angeles, Calif.)--Biography--Anecdotes. | Los Angeles (Calif.)--Biography--Anecdotes. | Administrative assistants--California--Los Angeles--Biography--Anecdotes. | Celebrities--California--Los Angeles--Anecdotes. | Event planners--California--Los Angeles--Biography--Anecdotes.
Classification: LCC F869.H74 F73 2019 | DDC 979.4/94053--dc23
LC record available at https://lccr.loc.gov/2019014377

Copyright 2019 by Jackie Frame

"Gal's, always keep a diary because one day it will keep you!"

Mae West

William Shakespeare said it best when he declared, "All the world's a stage and all the men and women merely players." I feel very blessed that on the stage I inhabited there were many, many players who performed major roles during my life and who helped to make it stimulating, glamorous and highly memorable. Everything quoted in this book can still be found in the hand-written notes in the diaries that I kept every day from 1957 to 1992. I sincerely hope that you enjoy these treasured memories.

Jackie Frame

List of Photographs

- A & M Group Photo with Herb Alpert (kneeling, front center) ...**215**
- AFI film cruise to Mexico in the early 70's with Olivia de Havilland, Glen Ford and director, King Vidor. ...**215**
- Angela Lansbury checking for her table number at an AFI Dinner. ...**216**
- Letter from Charlton Heston. ...**217**
- Debbie Reynolds enjoys the festivities at an AFI Dinner. ...**218**
- Letter from YPO after screening of Eartha Kitt movie. ...**219**
- Letter from director, Frank Capra. ...**220**
- Letter from Henry Fonda. ...**221**
- Letter from Jack Lemmon. ...**222**
- Poster from "The Sound of Music" autographed by Julie Andrews and director, Robert Wise. ...**223**
- Letter from LA Music Center - Center Theatre Group execs. Gordon Davidson and Charles Dillingham. ...**224**
- Letter from Stefanie Powers on behalf of the William Holden Wildlife Foundation. ...**225**
- From director, William Wyler. ...**226**

Contents

Chapter One:
Star Struck From The Very Beginning.. 1

Chapter Two:
The Big Decision 11

Chapter Three:
London To Los Angeles And All The "Firsts".. 19

Chapter Four:
The Music Business... 29

Chapter Five:
Socializing In The 70's... 47

Chapter Six:
The Exhausting, Exciting, and Educational 1980s 57

Chapter Seven:
In The Studio, Out Of Town, And On The Road! 95

Chapter Eight:
Behind The Scenes 117

Chapter Nine:
Togetherness... 135

Chapter Ten:
Difficult Challenges... 145

Chapter Eleven:
Close Encounters 157

Chapter Twelve:
Brief Encounters 187

Chapter Thirteen
'The Times They Are A-Changin' 205

List of Photographs.. 215

Index 227

Chapter One:
Star Struck From The Very Beginning

"So what took you to America?" asked Michael Caine (he wasn't Sir Michael in those days) over a glass of wine at the La Brea Inn in Hollywood, California. It was 1965 and probably the only justification for this circumstance was that we were both English!

I was a secretary at Liberty Records on Sunset Boulevard in Hollywood, and a man named Ron Kass was heading up its European Division under the EMI label in London. Ron would commute between the UK and the US and eventually go on to marry Joan Collins, but that's another story.

Ron Kass had spent some time in the UK, where he and Michael Caine had become friends, so when Michael made one of his early visits to Hollywood and didn't know many people, Ron thought I, being another Brit, would be a good candidate to entertain him! He asked if I would mind meeting Michael for a drink one evening, and of course I was thrilled to bits and, at the same time, sick with apprehension. Although Ron had given Michael my phone number, I really didn't think anything would come of it, but that evening in the apartment I shared with two English friends the phone rang. Shirley, one of my roommates, answered and when a voice asked for me, she replied in the usual fashion of the day, "May I tell her who's calling?" She nearly fell off her chair as she turned to me and mouthed Michael Caine!

Michael and I duly met for a drink at the La Brea Inn in Hollywood, just north of Sunset Boulevard. Michael had starred in *The Ipcress File* by then and had been nominated for a BAFTA award in the UK as Best Actor. But it wasn't until *Alfie* came out in 1966, the year after we met, that he really became a big name in the US.

On this occasion, in my early twenties and terribly nervous, I was consequently incredibly boring! Michael must have been cursing Ron for setting up our rendezvous. Adding to his misery was that he had spent the afternoon at a preview screening of *The Pawnbroker*, the first American movie to deal with the Holocaust from the viewpoint of a survivor, a German Jew tormented by horrendous memories of the deaths of his wife and children. After the war Rod Steiger's character opens a pawn shop in New York and exhibits his bitter and miserable outlook on life to everyone around him. Having taken in this most depressing, albeit excellent film, poor Michael must not have been in much of a mood to chat. However, his daughter was arriving the next day from England and he was taking her to Disneyland, which made for much happier conversation. He would have to hire a car and driver as he didn't drive at that time, so I offered to take him back to where he was staying, which I did. Although you couldn't call it an unequivocal success, it is always great dinner conversation when I say I had a date with Michael Caine.

All these years later, what can you say about Sir Michael Caine?! A star with one of the longest careers of all time and a myriad of awards, yet never becoming a victim of his own success. According to his biography, especially later in his acting life, he quite often only took on a role if he needed the money to re-decorate the dining room, buy another house, or just pay his income taxes!

Chapter One

I bumped into him several times over the years, once in the pet shop at the Beverly Center Shopping Mall in Los Angeles, and again at cocktail parties after various events. On one of these occasions, I reminded him of our "brief encounter" all those years before and he pretended to remember but I'm quite sure he did not.

On one particularly memorable occasion, during the American Film Institute's (AFI) salute to Lillian Gish in 1984, Michael proved his usual gallant and true English gentleman self. By that time I had started business for myself, having graduated from the ranks of secretary and personal assistant to being my own boss and handling various special events requiring professional treatment of all the logistics associated with major happenings. AFI was one notable client, and every year honored an individual from the film world fitting their criteria – "an individual whose talent has in a fundamental way advanced the film art; whose accomplishment has been acknowledged by scholars, critics, professional peers, and the general public; and whose work has stood the test of time."

Michael attended that dinner and was seated at a table adjacent to the steps leading up to the stage from where the very frail Miss Gish was to accept her award. For the presentation at the end of the evening she had to make her way from the head table in the center of the room through a throng of guests giving her a standing ovation. As she approached the stage, she hesitated at the obviously daunting steps to be climbed in a long gown with nothing to hold on to. Michael leapt to his feet and offered her his arm, which she most gratefully accepted, but I heard later that the producer of the show was most annoyed as it ruined the single shot he wanted of Lillian walking alone to the podium.

In answer to Michael's initial question as to what took me to the States, I explained it had been "a broken romance." That was only part of the reason, though. At the ripe old age of 22, I had long since despaired of the English climate as well as the direction in which I thought the country was going (I knew everything in those days), added to which I felt the lack of opportunity to do anything other than settle down in a semi-detached house and produce the inevitable 2.65 children, a prospect that held no appeal at all. It seemed to me the highlight of the week in that situation would be a barbecue in the back garden, *weather permitting*, and a discussion about what was on special at the local supermarket. Added to that would be an avid explanation of the route by which the guests had arrived at their destination, all of which sounded like a rather limiting prospective future! So I moved on.

* * * * *

Having been star struck for as long as I can remember prior to my departure for the US in 1964, I continued to pursue one of my favorite pastimes, which was the collection of autographs. With Jean, my best friend from school, we took great pride in getting through stage doors to meet our heroes! It was quite an art and we got very good at it. One of our earliest escapades took place at the London Palladium one of the most prominent variety theatres in the country.

Built in 1910 and located off Oxford Street in the heart of the West End of London, the roster of stars appearing on that famous stage included Judy Garland, Sophie Tucker, Bing Crosby, Danny Kaye, the Andrews Sisters, Bob Hope, Liza Minnelli, Ella Fitzgerald, Frank Sinatra, Sammy Davis, Jr., Frankie Laine, and Johnnie Ray. The Brits called it the American invasion, and it often meant the freezing out of many local stars of the day, who were relegated to second billing. But that did not prevent me from seeking autographs from all of them and as I quite rightly (in several instances) felt the second-billing stars would become first raters down the road.

In 1955 the Palladium was the setting for the top-rated English television variety show *Sunday Night at the London Palladium*, initially hosted by Tommy Trinder, an English stage, screen and radio comedian of the pre - and post-war years. At that time, his catchphrase "You lucky people" was bantered up and down the country. After that, Bruce Forsyth, a television presenter and entertainer, made the show his own and in the end was recognized by the *Guinness Book of World Records* as having the longest television career of any male entertainer. Broadcast live every week by ATV, I don't think I ever let a Sunday go by without watching.

Our method of entry for the collection of these signatory gems seemed to work best if we approached the usually inconspicuous stage door of the theatre, very often located down an obscure alley on the side or at the back of the building, with supreme confidence. There would usually be a little old man in a cubbyhole near the door peering through a grubby window, from which he would monitor the comings and goings of cast, crew, and fans. We would state in a seemingly well self-assured manner we were there to see whoever the star happened to be and generally would be waved in with complete indifference. At the Palladium on this occasion, our mark was Jerry Lewis, the American comedian and partner in comedic crime with Dean Martin. Sometimes we would be asked to give our names, but this time the old guy in charge wasn't the least bit interested and just let us through. We pretended to know where we were going, although in fact we didn't have a clue!

However, we walked smartly down the corridor until we saw a star on a dressing room door, which was usually a pretty safe bet.

Being relatively young and harmless as we were, most of the stars didn't seem to mind enthusiastic, unannounced fans intruding into their space, and we were able to get our autographs and sometimes even have a conversation. Jerry Lewis was affable enough and chatted along for a minute or two, but when we asked him to put "With love" on the page allocated for his signature, he said "Oh no, I can't do that, I keep my love just for my wife." Those were the days!!

* * * * *

Possibly our most successful "score" however, came in 1959, at the Finsbury Park Empire. This was another famous variety show venue, second only to the London Palladium. Although some American headliners were featured, more British stars called it home, including the legendary Gracie Fields and much-loved English comedian Tony Hancock.

Gracie Fields was a big name in England in the early half of the twentieth century and eventually headlined at the London Palladium over American import Eartha Kitt. She was always associated with the song "The Isle of Capri" and in fact retired there in her later years. Visitors would be invited to "have a cup of tea" if she was feeling up to it in her beloved villa *La Canzone Del Mare* overlooking the bay.

Tony Hancock was of the same era. An enormously popular comedian with a half hour radio show *Hancock's Half Hour,* he introduced it with almost a stutter emphasizing many more "H's" as he pronounced H...H...Hancock! The show ran for seven years. He was a household name appearing in numerous films and on stage. He had problems with alcohol and in 1968 committed suicide in Australia. He was not forgotten, however. In 2005 a poll to find the "Comedian's Comedian" voted him the 12th greatest comedian in the world.

In later years, more pop singers graced the stage of the Finsbury Park Empire, including Shirley Bassey, probably most famous for her rendition of "Goldfinger" from the James Bond film of the same name, and, although never recognized in the US, Alma Cogan, who was known as "The Girl With the Laugh/Giggle/Chuckle in Her Voice." Although the theatre no longer exists (a block of flats sits on its original location), it hosted my personal favorite, Cliff Richard, who appeared there in 1959 and became number one on my autograph hit list.

In those days it wasn't uncommon for unruly teenagers to tear up seats in cinemas where "Rock Around the Clock" featuring Bill Haley and His Comets, or some such film was playing, or riot outside theatres before and after shows. In fact I remember on one occasion in a state of delirious excitement screaming at the top of my lungs along with all the other fans and being told by a disgusted lady cop that we made her feel ashamed of her sex. Needless to say, I could not have cared less.

At the Finsbury Park Empire, appearing with his back-up group The Shadows, the show was sold out and the theatre filled with exuberant female fans screaming their heads off in appreciation of Cliff's vocal talents, not to mention his TDH looks (Tall, Dark & Handsome).

In this instance at the end of the show there was quite a bit of unruliness outside, but that didn't deter Jean and me from banging on the stage door to gain admittance. We obviously did a good job of giving the impression we were expected as, indeed, we ended up with Cliff (and others) in his dressing room. I remember he was absolutely charming and of course we both thought he was the most handsome young man we had ever met!! After chatting and getting his autograph in our books we tried to leave only to discover a riot going on outside.

"We are trapped!," I announced to Jean. "We can't leave, there's a riot outside!"

From then on, one of my most famous stories, of which I was inordinately proud and repeated over and over again, began with "when we were trapped in Cliff Richard's dressing room."

Many, many years later, in January 2010, Sir Cliff, as he had become by then, and I were passengers on the same cruise ship sailing from Fort Lauderdale through the Panama Canal to Los Angeles. I bumped into him in the ship's boutique one day, and he was as charming as ever and found my story of our first meeting all those years ago in Finsbury Park highly amusing. We also talked about tennis! Cliff has always been a great fan of the game, and I had grown up near Wimbledon and always tried to attend the famous Fortnight. I joked with him that, regrettable as it was, he just hadn't achieved the same amount of success in the US as in so many other places, so the only time American audiences saw him was during a rain delay on the Center Court at the Championships! He was very adept at leading all the spectators in song to pass the time. Of course, now there is a roof over the Center Court, so that won't happen again. I also bemoaned the loss of Andre Agassi, who had been my all-time favorite player and one of the people I regret never meeting. Sir Cliff agreed, and I remarked I had been given Agassi's new book, *Open*, as a Christmas gift. Cliff said he was looking forward to reading it himself. I got to thinking about that when I returned to my cabin and decided to lend him my book, as I hadn't even started it. I duly sent it off in a big envelope and the following day received it back again with a lovely note indicating he was right in the middle of something else but did appreciate my gesture. Also, he had a copy of "Open" waiting for him at home. Needless to say, to this day I use that thank you card as my permanent bookmark regardless of what I'm reading.

Chapter Two:
The Big Decision

But here's the answer to that very first question from Sir Michael Caine – What took me to America?

A lot of it was due to the fact that the phone didn't ring! It just sat there, a heavy black blob on the windowsill in the living room of the suburban bungalow I grew up in. Located in one of the home counties, Surrey, a mere 20-minute train ride from the center of London, it was considered a desirable area due to the commute distance, but I didn't appreciate that much and felt it was just plain boring! I was in my late teens at the time.

There were no answering machines or voice mail systems in those days, the redeeming feature for which was that you could always kid yourself that "he" had rung while you were out. Or maybe when you were talking to someone else, (no call waiting available either), so a good reason not to stay on the phone too long!

Of course, none of it did any good and however hard I looked at the black blob willing it to ring, it stayed silent. I have always been reminded of the wonderful Vikki Carr song "It Must Be Him," which I'm sure is true for all of us during those horrible days of realization that you have been dumped. The first time is the worst of all!

So – I ran away. I would come to realize as the years went by that after every traumatic event I would run away, but equally typically it would be somewhere exotic. I would be teased by my friends, who accused me of only disappearing to some isolated island or exciting city but always a very glamorous spot in which to suffer!

And so it was this first time – I ran away to Hollywood!

I had always had visions of going to America. I would watch Mary Tyler Moore on *The Dick Van Dyke Show* returning to her kitchen with multitudes of grocery bags, which she would dump on the counter distributing the contents into various cupboards and a huge refrigerator. I dreamed of doing the same thing one day. In the UK at that time, fridges were very small and you had to bend down to put things away and the so-called freezer was only big enough to carry one tiny metal ice tray which ended up encrusted and useless, as ice was rarely used in those days.

So, would it be New York, San Francisco, or Los Angeles? To me they were the three major cities from which to choose. All of 22 years old, and knowing only one person in the United States, Sue, a colleague with whom I had worked on a newspaper earlier in my career in London, made LA the preferred choice. Sue had moved to Hollywood the previous year and was working at Capitol Records just above Hollywood and Vine – what could possibly be more desirable!

The climate also had a lot to do with my decision, as it seemed California was the complete opposite of the UK. I used to laugh at the weather forecast in England, which seemed more or less the same every day: "Cloudy with bright intervals, rain at times." That didn't leave a lot out! Southern California however promised endless sunshine and much warmer climes.

The next step was to apply for a visa. I remember telephoning the American Embassy and stating my desire to visit the US for a three-month vacation to see how I liked it. I was told I would have to fill out an application, which they would send me, after which it would take several weeks to process. I would have to have a physical, and it would probably be two or three months before everything was completed.

Being in a state of emotional distress and also incapable of waiting for anything, another trait that would stick with me my entire life, I asked how I could cut corners. Not possible, I was told, to which I asked if I could at least go to the embassy to pick up the papers personally, thus avoiding a 2 to 3 day mail delivery (no computers in those days). They supposed that was OK so off I went up to Grosvenor Square, where the US Embassy was located until quite recently, to do just that. I was told this was all quite irregular, but nevertheless I received the paperwork and then, again in the name of expediency, I requested to fill in the forms there and then, thus avoiding another wait for the mail. Again, this was quite irregular, but they supposed that was OK, so I sat and filled in all the documents and left them at the Embassy. Already practically a week saved!

Next day I phoned and asked if they had been processed, knowing full well that would not be the case. Of course, no was the answer, so I said I would call every day to check and as soon as possible would like to come up for the physical as I was anxious to get to Los Angeles right away.

To cut a long story short, I made such a nuisance of myself that I was back there in less than a week, something that shouldn't have occurred for at least a month. During my interview, I was asked if I would like a Visitor or Immigration visa. What was the difference, I asked, to be told that if I took the Immigration variety I could work and earn some money. Well I thought that was a splendid idea as I would be there 3 months, and it made perfect sense to earn a little income.

So, a short time later, duly issued with a Green Card that had no expiration date and never required renewal, I got on the phone to Pan Am and booked a flight. I was in the States within three weeks of making my initial phone call.

* * * * *

The years leading up to my departure from the UK were spent in London offices most of the time, but usually at companies connected with show business. In those days it was very easy to flit from one job to another, and I probably turned down more than I accepted.

My very "first" was at the BBC in London in the late 1950s. I chose the BBC, not because of its prestigious name, although that was part of it, but mainly because they paid a salary based on qualifications, not age or previous experience. I was only 17 when I entered the work force, and other firms, like General Electric and Shell Oil, were influenced by years and previous employment history, of which apart from two days standing behind a counter in Woolworths, I had none! GE offered me 5 guineas a week (5 pounds sterling, and 5 shillings - neither guineas or shillings are in use today) but the BBC, based on my excellent shorthand and typing skills, offered me 7 pounds, 13 shillings and sixpence, representing a substantial difference to a young woman seeking financial independence, especially straight out of secretarial college. I did, however, have to borrow some money from my mother for the three-month season ticket on the train from New Malden to Waterloo, as the cost represented practically all my first month's salary!! It was quite a journey, looking back. No car at that time meant a walk of about half a mile from home to the bus stop, a 5-minute ride to the station and then 20 minutes on the train to Waterloo, usually standing most of the way. Then it was a bus or, if the queues were too long, a walk across Waterloo

Chapter Two

Bridge to Bush House in the Strand. I remember many times fighting off the wind and rain as I battled my way across the bridge. And all of this was before a start time of 9:00 am. It didn't seem difficult, because I didn't know any other way and everyone else was in the same boat!! I stayed with the BBC for several years and got my first taste of show business, beginning with radio at that time. Television existed then but I had not graduated to it. Those were the early days when the host of the BBC's popular panel game *What's My Line* Eamonn Andrews was also surprising celebrities and introducing them to *This Is Your Life*, a series which ran for many years. *What's My Line* was a panel game where contestants would answer questions about what they did for a living and the panel would guess their occupation. *This Is Your Life* would surprise a well known star led unsuspectingly into a theatre filled with a studio audience then presented him with family members and celebrity associates recounting their own personal stories.

A company called Morris Angel & Sons gave me my next job. They were theatrical costumiers and not very nice so moving on did not represent moving up. I didn't seem able to get along with my co-workers and bosses, and in the end was asked to give in my notice, but not before I had been able to take advantage of connections there to attend a Rock 'n' Trad Show at the Metropolitan theatre in the Edgeware Road. It was September 1960, and Billy Fury, a big star in the UK at that time, was one of the headliners. The audience was equally star studded. Sitting alongside me were Adam Faith, Jess Conrad, Lionel Bart (famous for writing *Oliver*), Marty Wilde, and Terry Dene, all major heartthrobs of the time.

A couple of other stints provided a rather dull existence so I returned to the music scene and began work as secretary to Maurice

Kinn, who founded the newspaper *New Musical Express*, and whose offices were located close to Soho and Denmark Street, known for its connections with the pop music scene as Tin Pan Alley due to its large concentration of shops selling musical instruments. I had been a longtime reader before working there and couldn't wait for its delivery every Friday to see who had made it to Number One on the Hit Parade.

In the early 1950s, Soho had become the center of the beatnik culture in London, housing the famous 2i's Coffee Bar, probably the first rock club in Europe at 59 Old Compton Street. It soon became the center of the fledgling rock scene in London. Soho's Wardour Street was the home of the legendary Marquee Club, which opened in 1958, and where the Rolling Stones first performed in July 1962. Coffee bars such as Le Macabre, which had coffin-shaped tables, fostered beat poetry, jive dance, and political debate. It was a very *cool* scene and I felt very *in with the in crowd* to be frequenting such a neighborhood.

Soho was not a suitable area after dark, at least not for the likes of me, as it was reputed to be a base for the sex industry – a red light district, one might say. But being so close to the 2i's coffee bar, affectionately referred to as "the birthplace of British Rock'n Roll," I would often stop in during daylight hours very often at lunchtime to star gaze. Tommy Steele was known to frequent the place. I never saw him there, but did meet and chat to his brother Colin Hicks one day along with Screaming Lord Sutch, the man who founded the Official Monster Raving Loony political party. But it was Tommy Steele I really wanted to see. He was a big star at that time, having reached number one with "Singing the Blues" (covered in the US by Guy Mitchell) in 1957, and *The Tommy Steele Story* was the first album by a UK act to reach number one. His film credits would include *Half a Sixpence*, *The Happiest*

Millionaire, and *Finian's Rainbow*, but like so many British stars he never really made it big in the US.

London was fun in those days, though living in the suburbs and working in the West End was not totally conducive to taking advantage of all the arts and entertainment available. Many a time I would have to leave a theatre before the end of the third act in order to catch the last train home, otherwise it would be the milk train at 5am. Then as now, living in town was very expensive so I had to put up with the inconvenience of missing out on a few things so that I could continue living within my means.

Chapter Three:
London To Los Angeles And All The "Firsts"

All this led to life in the United States.

The aphorism "There's a first time for everything" proved to be only too true after I emerged from my Pan Am flight from London to Los Angeles to embark on the next phase of my life. Of course, age has a lot to do with "firsts," but I like to think that's not necessarily a barrier and that an equally rewarding first time experience can occur at any age. This would prove to be true. However, I do believe the "first" time for anything is usually the most memorable!

I arrived on June 17, 1964, and from the very beginning I was part of legendary Hollywood. I stayed with my friend Sue from newspaper days in London, and discovered that she lived in the Alto Nido apartments at the very top of Vine Street, right above the famous intersection of Hollywood and Vine. William Holden's character is seen living in this complex at the beginning of the 1950 film *Sunset Boulevard*.

My initial weekend was full of "firsts" and very exciting to me. I couldn't believe I was actually in Los Angeles, walking down Hollywood Boulevard, head bent and eyes glued to my feet reading all the names of the stars as I strode along the famous Walk of Fame!

Apart from my "first" trek down Hollywood Boulevard examining the stars along the sidewalk displaying celebrity names, the world famous Sunset Strip also beckoned. One Saturday night a group of us went to the Whisky A Go Go, where Johnny Rivers was performing. It's not common knowledge that Johnny Rivers collaborated on writing the theme song for a British television series *Danger Man* starring Patrick McGoohan, which was shown in the US as *Secret Agent*. The Johnny Rivers recording of "Secret Agent Man" sold a million copies and put him firmly in rock star category. Johnny was a popular favorite at that time with celebrities from other genres, as well as his own fans. One evening, his audience included Steve McQueen and Ty Hardin. Steve McQueen was well on his way up the stardom ladder, having completed *The Great Escape*, Hollywood's fictional depiction of the true story of a historical mass escape from a German POW camp in World War II. Another memorable contribution of his came when he starred with Natalie Wood in *Love with the Proper Stranger*. Ty Hardin was not as well known, but had gained a strong following when he took over from Clint Walker in the television series *Cheyenne*. We weren't that interested in their credits, however. The fact that both were gorgeous and TDH (tall, dark and handsome) was enough!

More "firsts" would prove less successful, including my initial try for an American driver's license. Although I had a car in England and had driven all over France and Spain, I had to take the test locally. The first time I failed dismally, which I found very annoying based on my past experience, but all was redeemed on my second attempt, despite a thoroughly unpleasant and difficult examiner.

Years later, although still a "first" I had a telephone installed in my car, a Chrysler LeBaron. It was October 13, 1987 and a very elaborate operation. I remember it took the guy about two hours to put equipment between the front seats and then get the telephone within reach. It was reassuring to have it despite an installation fee of about $200.

On Sunday, October 4, 1964, I went to the Hollywood Bowl for the "first" time. Billed as a "No on Proposition 14 Rally," it was a star-studded gathering of the biggest names in the industry. Proposition 14 would have nullified the Rumford Fair Housing Act, which had passed in 1963 to help end racial discrimination by property owners who refused to rent or sell to African-Americans. Urging the audience to vote no were Elizabeth Taylor, Richard Burton, Gregory Peck, Yul Brynner, Nat "King" Cole, Dick van Dyke, Henry Mancini, Joey Bishop, Milton Berle, The Kingston Trio, the McGuire Sisters, Nancy Wilson, James Garner, and Burt Lancaster! I chose quite a night!

A different kind of "first" at the Bowl would come many years later, in 1976, when after forty years of performances, the concert was rained out. And would you believe I had tickets for that night. That was certainly a "first" I could have lived without!

Previews and opening nights of movies were quite commonplace in Hollywood, but not for me, so I was thrilled to attend my "first" premiere, on October 28, 1964, at the Egyptian Theatre on Hollywood Boulevard. Opened in 1922, Grauman's, as it was then called (having been built by a man named Sid Grauman), quickly became a famous landmark. The Hollywood premiere of *Robin Hood* starring Douglas Fairbanks had recently been held there, and it became home to many glittering evenings over the years.

The film I saw that night was *My Fair Lady* and the audience included its stars, Audrey Hepburn and Rex Harrison, as well as Frank Sinatra *with* Natalie Wood (note *with*, which gave the columnists something to talk about), singers Dean Martin and Andy Williams, comedienne Lucille Ball, funnyman Danny Thomas, columnist Hedda Hopper, television personality from *77 Sunset Strip* Efrem Zimbalist, Jr, *A Summer Place's* Troy Donohue, and more in the TDH group with Steve McQueen and Tab Hunter. What a glittering show that "first" was!

Just along the road was another spectacular theatre also named after Mr. Grauman – it began as Grauman's Chinese and went on to be renamed Mann's Chinese. It is most famous for the "Hand and Footprints" on the pavement in front of the building. Norma Talmadge is credited with being the initial contributor, when by accident in 1927 she stepped into wet concrete. Miss Talmadge's main claim to fame however had come in 1923, when a poll of picture exhibitors named her the number one box office star. She was earning $10,000 a week, a far cry from the $25 she had been receiving in 1911 for playing bit parts. After wildly successful silent films, including the most popular of her entire career, *Smilin' Through*, one of the greatest screen romances of the silent film era, her career faltered when talkies came in so she went on to become a successful business woman.

Another famous landmark was the Hollywood Palladium. My "first" time there was to a charity concert on Sunday, November 15, 1964, and I must admit to having no interest at all in the charity involved. But Frank Sinatra was appearing in the show, and that was all I cared about! There was a dinner as well as entertainment, and a group of five of us managed to get on a table quite close to the stage to enjoy the festivities. As well as Frank, who was incredible of course, the Four Freshmen, Morey Amsterdam, Dinah Shore, George Shearing, Henry Mancini, Andy Williams, the Osmond Brothers, Joey Bishop, June Christie, Dean Martin, and Peggy Lee took their turns. I was really seeing Hollywood in style.

But back to those very early days right after I set foot on US soil, on one of which, Sue and I went to a coffee shop for lunch on Hollywood Boulevard, where I had cream cheese and bagels for the "first" time – all very American to me – and even the coffee shop seemed different from anything I had experienced in England. We bumped into a colleague of hers from another record label (Sue worked at Capitol Records), and he mentioned perhaps being of help to me in the job market as he was currently employed at Vee Jay Records, where the Vice President was looking for a new secretary. He suggested I apply. I happily agreed, thinking that regardless of the outcome it would be another interesting experience. The interview was set up for the next day, and before I left the apartment, Sue gave me a few pointers. I was to make sure I maintained my English accent, which wouldn't be difficult as I had only just got "off the boat" so to speak, and if asked what sort of salary I expected I should say $450 a month. I could always come down, Sue informed me. She was currently making $375 after a year at Capitol and she got a free record album of her choice every month. It seemed like a fortune to me.

I duly reported to the office of VP Jay Lasker the following day primed and ready. Lasker was straight out of central casting as far as I was concerned. Somewhat rotund, he was seated behind a huge desk, leaning back in a swivel chair with a large cigar protruding from his mouth. "So you want to be a stenographer?," he announced in rather grand style. Since I had absolutely no idea what that was I had to enquire as to the definition of a stenographer? This seemed to amuse and delight him no end. Anyway, nothing put him off. He was, as expected, charmed by the accent and offered me the job right away. "How much money do you want, honey?," he asked, to which I replied right on cue, "Four hundred and fifty dollars a month." "Fine," he said, "when can you start." Sue was furious when I got back to think I was making so much more money than she. Needless to say, I started work the very next day. Thus began my working career in the United States.

In those early days Vee-Jay was flying high with huge financial success coming from the first of the Beatles' hits. Although the group had transferred its allegiance to Capitol by the time I got there, Vee-Jay had already released two albums that included earlier songs like "Please, Please Me," "Twist And Shout," "I Saw Her Standing There," and "Do You Want To Know A Secret." Every Friday evening about 6 o'clock they would have a champagne party to celebrate all this success. It was like a whole new world to me, and I loved every minute of it.

I made all the usual foreign *faux pas*, and on one memorable occasion during my first week I went into the storeroom to request some additional stationary supplies, where a very cute guy named George was in charge. Requesting a shorthand notebook, pens, and paper clips I added I would also need some pencils and a rubber! For the uninitiated, a "rubber" in England is used to erase mistakes written in pencil, but in the States a "rubber" is slang for "condom." I was used to rubbing out mistakes with its namesake, and would never have dreamt of using the word "eraser." The poor guy turned beet red and was thoroughly embarrassed. I didn't know what I'd said, but never made that mistake again.

Another truly significant "first" took place on Monday, August 24, 1964, when the Beatles arrived in the US for their initial appearances. It was shortly after I had moved to Los Angeles, and it was a red-letter day for any number of people, certainly the pop music fans who adored them, but also for my friend Sue who was working for their label,

Capitol Records. She was very involved in the welcome party Capitol was giving them, which she *had* to attend. When she came home, she reported they were all very nice, very down to earth, and not the least blasé about anything! I don't think she realized she was the envy of so many people at the time, including me, and as with most fans we all had our favorites. Mine was Paul McCartney. We are exactly the same age, Paul's birthday is in May, and mine in April, so I felt a bit like a kindred spirit although regrettably, even though I came close, I never actually met him. Maybe there is still time.

Many years later, when I had switched my allegiance from the record business to the film industry and was working at The American Film Institute, AFI had a truly memorable "first."

Over the weekends of April 28/29 and May 3/4, 1975, AFI held an Open House at Greystone Mansion in Beverly Hills. The event was the brainchild of then Director of AFI West, Martin Manulis, a prolific television, film, and theatre producer, probably best known for the film *The Days of Wine and Roses*, starring Jack Lemmon and Lee Remick.

The event was designed to draw attention to AFI's existence, which at that time was a sort of question mark. It seemed no one really knew what AFI was all about. On their official website, it said the purpose and programs included a promise "to preserve the history of the motion picture, to honor the artists and their work and to educate the next generation of storytellers."

Within the organization the educational Conservancy took pride of place. Classes in cinematography, directing, editing, producing, production design, and screenwriting allowed students, known as Fellows, to learn their craft in a hands-on production environment with an emphasis on storytelling.

All this was a bit difficult for the general public to grasp or truthfully to be that interested in. It was decided therefore, to send invitations to a massive event covering two consecutive weekends at Greystone, where they could tour the building, which had its own unique history, view any number of student films, check out the Library, look at the hidden bar in the bowling alley basement (used in the days of prohibition by the Doheny family and where many of the student films were shot), and in general get to know what was happening. And it was free!

It was a huge task just getting the program coordinated as well as sending out thousands of invitations and generating publicity so that the maximum number of guests would attend.

Many visitors were hoping to see movie stars, of course, and they weren't disappointed. On the first day Charlton Heston, famous in many roles including *Ben-Hur*, for which he received the Academy Award, was very much present and very gracious in meeting, greeting, and promoting the cause! George Peppard, probably best known for his role opposite Audrey Hepburn in *Breakfast at Tiffany's*, put in an appearance, and on subsequent days Karl Malden, best-known as television's Lt. Mike Stone in *The Streets of San Francisco*, stopped by. Dana Andrews, whose movie *The Best Years of Our Lives* had received great critical acclaim, was joined by Ricardo Montalban who would become the star of TV's *Fantasy Island,* as well as English actor Michael York, of *Cabaret* fame.

Everyone who came seemed to enjoy the occasion, but whether it generated the desired interest and recognition was a moot point. From my point of view, it was tremendous fun but working long hours for three straight weeks and two weekends with not a moment to relax

Chapter Three

proved exhausting. I don't think I've appreciated a Friday night as much as I did when, finally, a weekend off loomed on the horizon.

In May 1977 a second Open House was held, but over only one weekend instead of two, and with over 3,000 people the first day and even more on the Sunday. It was a great success. Celebrity input was as strong as ever, with the hits of Saturday being Robert Wagner and Natalie Wood and, on Sunday, Gregory Peck, Lucille Ball, and Henry Fonda, joined by Fellows from the Conservatory who, although not as recognizable, were, or would become, integral parts of the film world.

In 1975 the US Post Office issued the first and only D.W. Griffith stamp commemorating that great director's work on such early classic films as *The Birth of a Nation* (1915) and, subsequently, *Intolerance*, starring his frequent leading lady Lillian Gish. AFI arranged an evening at Greystone to celebrate this event and Miss Gish, together with Gregory Peck, were both on hand to act as hosts. The two of them would each go on to receive their own accolades, being honored with AFI's Life Achievement Award in 1984 and 1989, respectively.

At small intimate gatherings like these I observed legendary figures, and even get to know some of them, at least slightly, which helped my working relationship on future events and made us all a little more comfortable.

Perhaps the most famous and enduring organization in the film industry is AMPAS – the Academy of Motion Picture Arts and Sciences. Formed in 1927 by Louis B. Mayer, it had been in existence for many years and was best known for the annual Oscars presentation ceremony. Tickets to attend the Academy Awards were virtually impossible to come by unless you were a nominee, but one rather spectacular event I was able to attend was the opening of the Academy's brand-new headquarters on Wilshire Boulevard in Beverly Hills in December 1975. A series of grand opening parties were held for Academy members, prominent civic leaders, the press corps, and rich and famous people from far and wide. Special screenings in the Samuel Goldwyn Theater of clips from past Academy Award-winning Best Pictures reminded us of the legacy. Oscar-winning stars became very special guests over the course of several evenings, and searchlights outside the theatre could be seen for miles around.

Through my association with AFI, I had been invited to the opening night, which was a black-tie affair. I would have loved to have gone, but unfortunately, I had no escort available at that time with a tux (nor the means to rent one - still the poverty stricken out-of-work actor syndrome, I suppose). But I was able to attend one of the parties later in the week, where everything was pretty much the same except no black-tie was required. On that occasion my date was John Cooke, Alistair Cooke's son. He was a folk singer, which was presumably why he didn't have formal wear for the celebration on the first night. Alistair Cooke, although a renowned journalist in the UK, was best known in the US for being the host of PBS's Masterpiece Theatre, a position he held for twenty-two years starting in 1971. In retrospect I would have thought he had an old tux he could have handed down but again, maybe a folk singer just wouldn't be caught dead wearing one!

So began my career in the entertainment world, which would lead me into all the other fields of "the business," as it remains known. From music, film, theatre, dance, and television – all the stars would come to my party!

Chapter Four:
The Music Business

The 1960s held highly memorable musical events for me. One such evening took place in the Hollywood Hills at a very fancy dinner party honoring a visiting celebrity. I had received an invitation but wasn't quite sure why, and when I got there I was mistaken for somebody else.

The occasion was to welcome British singer Matt Monro, known as "The Man With The Golden Voice," to the US and to California, where he planned to relocate. His record company threw a party to introduce him to some local big wigs and although I was unsure why I was on the guest list, I had been a fan for years in England and was delighted at the thought of meeting him in person.

The evening did not start well. My date and I got lost in the twisting streets where Hollywood Boulevard becomes residential and winds carelessly into the hills west of Laurel Canyon. We finally arrived not fashionably late, but very late indeed. In fact the cocktail hour was well and truly over and everyone had taken their seats at the place-carded tables by the time we got there. "Oh, we're so glad you made it," gushed the host, "we've been waiting for you, come in, come in." Thoroughly surprised and somewhat embarrassed by this elaborate greeting, we didn't have time to apologize for being late or that we weren't who they obviously thought we were before we were ushered into the private dining room and seated with Mr. Monro himself. Guests not among the chosen few were seated elsewhere scattered throughout the house, and to this day I have no idea who I was thought to be, but it was a wonderful evening and Matt was a total delight.

"The singing bus driver," as he was affectionately known in England (in one of his earlier careers he had driven a London bus), he was to go on to much bigger and better things, recording highly memorable songs like *Softly As I Leave You* and *Portrait of my Love*. He went on to record *From Russia with Love* from the James Bond movie, *Born Free* from the film of the same name, and the Beatles' *Yesterday*, adding to a long list of classic hits.

His career faltered somewhat in his later years, but I always felt he should have maintained the critical acclaim he so deserved. No example of that was more evident than when I saw him in concert on the Isle of Wight off the south coast of England. I was on holiday visiting family when I saw a poster advertising his shows on the end of the pier in the seaside town of Sandown, where he was performing twice nightly, at 5:45pm and again at 9:15pm. Together with my retired aunt and uncle, who had recently moved to the Island and who were not the least bit interested in pop singers, we went to the early show. We sat at the back of the stalls, and to my amazement there were fewer than a dozen people in the entire audience. It was a big theatre, and as Matt came on stage and looked out at us he quipped, "I think we should change places there's more of us on stage than there are in the audience!" I moved from the back to the front row and remember seeing a spectacular performance. It was as if he were singing to a sold-out house in a prestigious Las Vegas show room. He was totally professional and completely oblivious to the current rather sad surroundings, giving this lucky audience a thoroughly polished and perfect performance.

Chapter Four

* * * * *

Years earlier even before I had left the UK I was in the audience to see a new musical. It was Thursday, September 14, 1961, and I watched Anthony Newley and Leslie Bricusse's new show *Stop the World - I Want to Get Off!* at the Queen's Theatre in London. The show included some of the most popular songs of that generation, which are still heard to this day. "What Kind of Fool Am I" and "Gonna Build a Mountain" were destined to be recorded by dozens of artists all over the globe for many years thereafter.

The first time I met Anthony Newley was in a recording studio at A&M Records. It was in the early 1970s, and he was with his third wife, former airline stewardess Dareth Rich. I was working at A&M at the time and remember staying late when I knew he would be recording so I could finally get to meet him. I wasn't at all disappointed. He was friendly and down to earth and, as I always seemed to find when meeting a fellow Brit, an invisible connection was apparent, based I quite firmly believe on our unique sense of humor.

Years later in London, he was appearing at a nightclub in the West End when I was vacationing there, so I went to see his cabaret act. Newley was a good friend and associate of friends in Los Angeles who were also in London and had some papers they wanted to get to him. Knowing that I would be attending the show that evening, they asked if I would mind going backstage after his performance to deliver them. I was thrilled at another opportunity to say hello, needless to say. The performance that night was particularly memorable because of his opening – he walked out across the stage and everyone expected him to stop at the microphone and start his act. But instead, he kept walking past the mike, off the stage through the audience seated at their tables, and looking neither to the left or right, without any hesitation kept on going, past the exit sign and through the door out to the street! Everyone was so taken aback it took a few seconds to realize he would of course return, which he did but it was one of the most spectacular ways to open an act I had ever seen. With Mr. Newley's sense of humor, no one should really have been surprised at all. At the end of the evening I gave him the envelope as requested, for which he was most grateful.

*****

After being fired from Liberty Records because I took an unauthorized vacation, I moved on to A&M. In my defense, I should add I had booked a week's holiday in Hawaii to take my mother, who would be visiting from England, as a surprise Mother's Day present. I wasn't about to forfeit that, job or no job.

My sojourn to the Hawaiian Islands was a most successful escapade, and upon my return I went about creating three more great firsts. It was 1967. My wonderful new job at A&M Records began, and I bought my first new car. It was a white MGB convertible for which I paid the princely sum of $1,000. I literally drove it off the showroom floor. I felt like Vanessa Redgrave when she played Isadora Duncan with my white chiffon scarf blowing in the wind and thought I was the bee's knees. Of course, I had to find suitable accommodation, which necessitated a garage, so the third first was a new place to live. Duly having accomplished that, and with the MG happily and securely ensconced in its new home, I began work at A&M. I sold that car ten years later when it needed new brakes and a multitude of other repairs for the same $1,000 I paid for it!

A&M Records was housed in the old Charlie Chaplin Studios at 1416 North La Brea Avenue, just south of Sunset Boulevard in

Hollywood. The name came from the initials of Herb Alpert and Jerry Moss, and the company thrived from 1966 to 1999. Apart from Herb Alpert and the Tijuana Brass, other prominent artists included the Carpenters, Burt Bacharach, Quincy Jones, Procol Harum, Liza Minnelli, Paul Williams, Joan Baez, Cat Stevens, and Joe Cocker.

In the 1970s, A&M was one of the most successful companies in the recording business. Of course, Herb Alpert and the Tijuana Brass had countless hits (who can forget "The Lonely Bull") and helped bring them to prominence, but there were any number of other artists like the Carpenters' with "We've Only Just Begun," Procol Harum's "A Whiter Shade of Pale," and Joe Cocker's "You Are So Beautiful," all contributing to years of enduring success.

For five years, I was Jerry Moss's assistant. He was one of the nicest, most considerate, and wonderful bosses I ever had. He always appreciated his good fortune and never took it for granted. In a fit of sheer extravagance, he did buy a Rolls Royce, but had to have a lemon painted on the side, as it was constantly in the shop. He was tempted to get a second so he could have one facing in each direction when the other one wasn't there. He was also very romantic, and I remember his wife Sandy's 40th birthday, on which he had roses delivered in a big truck to their house. Not content with forty red roses, he had forty *dozen* delivered, hence the need for the truck.

There was a big difference in those days working in the US as opposed to the UK. When I was at the BBC in London, we would have breaks in the mornings and afternoons when ladies with trolleys would come round selling coffee, tea, and buns. In the US there was usually a coffee room, where a constant supply seemed to be available all day with never a thought of paying for it. One day another employee was there and grumbling profusely at the quality of the coffee and she got the sharp edge of my tongue as I told her in no uncertain terms that "the price was right wasn't it" and under the circumstances she should be appreciative, not critical. She had no idea how lucky she was.

Another extravagance in which Jerry Moss indulged was horse racing - not just going to the track, but having his very own race horses. This was something he had in common with Burt Bacharach, and at one time they had several horses between them. One afternoon in February 1970, Jerry's horse Angeltune was running at Santa Anita. I remember placing a $2 bet with him as he left the office and was highly delighted when he returned and gave me $23! Many years later in 2005 his horse Giacomo would win the Kentucky Derby, but I hadn't had an opportunity to place a bet that time.

During my time at A&M, one of the most surprising success stories was when Herb's rendition of an old Burt Bacharach song found hidden under countless papers at the bottom of a desk drawer rocketed to No. 1 on the Billboard charts. Everyone at the company was thrilled for Herb as we were all a little bit in love with him because he was such a dashing, if very shy, and extraordinarily handsome young man. I remember the day "This Guy's In Love With You" hit the number one spot. I was sitting at my desk and Herb came through the door with a big smile on his face. We all congratulated him on his success (because equally we all knew but never admitted, that he really couldn't sing a note) and he said, "you don't have to be nice to me just because I own the door!" and of course we all burst out laughing assuring him that was not the case.

Burt's input at A&M had nothing to do with horses, however. His contribution in the form of many classic songs was much more important. I don't know who holds the record for writing the most hit songs, but Burt has to be close to the top. Apart from "Raindrops Keep Falling on my Head," there was "Alfie," "Do You Know the Way to San Jose," "The Look of Love," "I'll Never Fall in Love Again," and the immortal "That's What Friends are For." It's too bad Burt doesn't have the most appealing singing voice in the world, but he made up for it though by being so talented, not to mention charming and gorgeous.

In 1969 Burt had won an Oscar for "Raindrops Keep Falling On My Head," his number one hit from *Butch Cassidy and the Sundance Kid*. I wrote him a note offering my congratulations and to my surprise he wrote back. That note became the first of a collection of treasured cards and letters received over the years.

Sergio Mendes and Brasil 66 were on the label at that time, with Lani Hall their lead singer. After a scandalous liaison (or so it seemed to us) with Claudine Longet (Andy Williams's wife), Herb Alpert and Lani Hall became an item, and rumor had it there was a wedding dress in her closet just waiting for the right moment to get married. In 1974 the right moment arrived and, as the saying goes, "the rest is history."

Karen and Richard Carpenter became the most successful singing duo at A&M Records in the 1970s. The two of them would often come to see Jerry, and while waiting on the couch in the outer office, we would chat. I remember Karen was never completely happy with her image and felt she wasn't glamorous enough for the stage. That's possibly why she preferred being at the back behind the drums rather than performing out front. I don't think she realized just how talented she was, nor as songwriter Paul Williams would always say, that "she had the voice of an angel."

Also at A&M the same time as The Carpenters, was Paul Williams himself. He was one of the most gifted songwriters of the 20th century, but as with most "behind the scenes" artists, he wasn't a household name, unlike those who sang his songs. Barbra Streisand for instance immortalized "Evergreen" from the movie *A Star Is Born*, for which Paul wrote the lyrics to her music, and they won an Oscar. But it was really his association with the Carpenters that put him on the map with classics like "We've Only Just Begun" and "Rainy Days and Mondays."

Then he went on to write "Rainbow Connection" for *The Muppet Movie,* which garnered more attention while a varied collection of artists recorded his songs over the years. Three Dog Night's "An Old Fashioned Love Song" and Helen Reddy's "You and Me Against the World" became major hits. Another connection once removed was his composition of "The Love Boat," the theme of the eponymous television show, sung by Jack Jones.

I first met Paul at a party in 1971, and in 1972 he played at The Troubadour in Los Angeles on a double bill with Helen Reddy. I recall thinking he was great, although Helen wasn't as good as the first time I had seen her!

Many years later in January 2010, Paul was one of the guest entertainers on the cruise ship Seabourn Odyssey's Maiden World Voyage from Fort Lauderdale to Athens. I got to know him better during that time, together with his wife Mariana, and we reminisced about the A&M days over lunch one day with Cruise Director Barry Hopkins. Cliff Richard was also a passenger and sitting at an adjoining table. Remembering Cliff at the Finsbury Park Empire when we were both teenagers, I felt I'd come full circle. Paul sang many of his hits on that cruise and was very popular with the guests, although by his own admission he's not a singer. That didn't matter; his shows brought back wonderful memories for everyone.

"We've Only Just Begun" was one of a string of hits showcasing Karen Carpenter's extraordinary voice. It began as a television commercial for Crocker National Bank and forever after became the favorite song played at weddings.

Karen and Richard Carpenter's first album *Offering* included a re-working of the Beatles "Ticket to Ride" sung slowly by Karen with a completely new and different arrangement by brother Richard. Herb Alpert is given credit on the album cover as "Shaker: H. Alpert." However, it was their second hit, "(They Long To Be) Close to You," from the Burt Bacharach and Hal David team, that propelled them firmly into the limelight.

In 1974, The Carpenters album *Horizon* was released. The song that to me represented Karen the most (although written for a man) was "Desperado." Don Henley of the Eagles is credited with writing it and the lyrics, including the lines *"And freedom, oh freedom, well that's just some people talkin'/You're a prisoner walkin' through this world all alone,"* could well be describing how Karen felt about her life. Although she married, it wasn't a success and she was due to sign divorce papers the day she died.

Although it seemed they had everything, Karen always seemed to be battling something and was never really satisfied with the way things were working out. I think she may have had low self-esteem, and word has it someone told her she was fat once. True or not, she always worried about her weight and appearance. According to one source, at age 17 she lost twenty pounds on the Stillman Diet. Although that was with a doctor's guidance, weight loss haunted her for the rest of her life. Her tragic death in 1983 brought the horrors of anorexia to the fore as the music world lost one of the most beautiful voices ever heard. It was almost as if she had lived out another Don Henley song – "Hotel California," whose lyrics include the lines:

> "Last thing I remember, I was
> Running for the door
> I had to find the passage back
> To the place I was before
> "Relax, " said the night man,
> "We are programmed to receive.
> You can check-out any time you like,
> But you can never leave! "

* * * * *

Then there was Joe Cocker!

Joe had a unique way with a song and had perfect pitch. He was also a muddle. When I knew him, he was recording for A&M and would have frequent meetings with Jerry Moss.

During one of our conversations, he told me if he hadn't been able to release his pent up emotions with his singing, he would probably have been a murderer! Whether of course that would have been true we will never know, but fortunately the Joe I met back then was a simple, gentle soul who, by his own admission, wasn't overly intelligent, but neither was he by any means stupid. An example of that came to light when word went round there was an outstanding royalty check that had never been cashed which it seemed was payable to Joe Cocker. According to the inside gossip Joe had been carrying it around in his shirt pocket for months not knowing quite what to do with it. One thing he did know was he didn't trust anyone in his own entourage and therefore knew better than to hand it over to any one of them. By the same token, he didn't have a bank account he knew of in the US so what to do? In the end, of course, it all got sorted out, but I often wonder what he did with all that money.

Joe's whole life had centered round music and he played and sang in various bands in and around Sheffield, England, where he grew up, before finally entering the big time in the US with a groundbreaking rearrangement of The Beatles song "With a Little Help from My Friends." He sang at Woodstock in August 1969, where he and the Grease Band had to be flown into the festival by helicopter because the crowd was so huge that travel on the ground became impossible. The mud caused by inclement weather didn't help, either.

The year 1969 was significant in the world of music thanks to Woodstock marching firmly into the history books. Officially named the Woodstock Music & Arts Fair, but almost always referred to as just "Woodstock," it was to be "An Aquarian Exposition: 3 Days of Peace & Music" on a dairy farm in the Catskills from August 15 to 17. Despite a rainy weekend, it ran over an extra day as thirty-two acts performed outdoors before an audience of 400,000. It was a pivotal moment in popular music history, and *Rolling Stone* listed it as one of the "50 Moments That Changed the History of Rock and Roll."

After Woodstock, Joe's second album was released. The Beatles were so impressed by his cover of "With a Little Help from My Friends" that they allowed him to include their songs "She Came in Through the Bathroom Window" and "Something." Later Billy Preston's "You Are So Beautiful" became another classic Joe could call his own when he included it in *I Can Stand a Little Rain* in 1974.

In the early days at A&M, Joe had a lot of problems, one of which was alcohol abuse. To his frequent meetings with Jerry Moss he always came in with a paper bag in hand. He would wait on the couch in the outer office chatting with me, now and then taking a swig before entering the inner sanctum. Jerry asked me once if I would make sure he got rid of the paper bag before these meetings. I couldn't figure out a way to do that so never did.

Joe had terrible teeth, which being English came as no surprise in those days. Growing up in the north of England and at the mercy of Britain's National Health Service, Joe was not alone when it came to this problem and had certainly never been to a dentist in his life by the look of his teeth at that time. One day during a meeting (complete with the paper bag I had not been able to persuade him to part with) Joe must have complained about something relating to his mouth, because Jerry came out and asked me if I knew a good dentist. I said yes and the next thing I knew I had been assigned to take Joe to Century City for an appointment. I remember walking along Century Park East feeling rather incongruous beside him with his wild hair and, even when not on stage, idiosyncratic arm movements. Several months later when keeping my own cleaning appointment, my dentist made me promise never to refer anyone to him again, as he said he had never seen a mouth or teeth in such terrible shape. I imagine the bill, which was sent to A&M, had substantially increased his income for that year.

In his later years, Joe moved to Colorado where he died of lung cancer in 2014. Even though he had probably mellowed by then, I feel sure he was still a unique personality.

* * * * *

Not only were there legendary performers in the 1970s, there were legendary sites as well, and none was better known than the Santa Monica Pier. In those days the first thing you saw upon entering the Pier was a Carousel known as the Merry-Go-Round featuring forty-four hand-carved horses. Complete with appropriate musical accompaniment, these sturdy steeds never got tired of gracefully prancing up and down on a never-ending round of pleasure to the delight of their riders. A small number of apartments were housed within and it was considered particularly glamorous and "hip" to live there!

On the evening of Saturday, April 22, 1972, I was invited to a party by a colleague from A&M who lived in one of these apartments on the pier. It was appropriately decorated in the "hippie" fashion of the day, with cushions on the floor and lots of candles and throws all over the place. Thick with smoke most of the time from goodness knows what, the night I was there one of the other guests who could not have fit the scene better was Joan Baez. "One Of The Most Distinctive Voices Of The Folk Rock Era" best described Joan as she began her career in the late 1950s.

Being a part of Woodstock helped propel Joan into the international music world, where she began writing many of her own songs, including "A Song For David," for her then husband David Harris. She appeared frequently at various venues around Los Angeles. After one such concert at UCLA, I was heard to remark her songs were great, but she got a bit boring once she got started on her political beliefs. So much for my general interest in anything of a serious nature, but then I was still fairly young at the time.

In 2012 I read a biography of Apple's genius CEO Steve Jobs and was interested to see that Joan had at one time been his girlfriend. He could have been with her at that party for all I knew, as I wouldn't have recognized him, although I was always a Mac freak and point blank refused ever to use a PC. Those apartments on the pier are long gone now, but if walls could talk, what a history they would have been able to reveal.

Joan became a household name for decades, both in the music field and the political arena.

* * * * *

All my life people have been known to say I remind them of Julie Andrews. I'm flattered of course, even though my ability to sing is nonexistent. However, I do admit to a very slight similarity from a physical standpoint as we are the same height and our haircuts during *The Sound of Music* days were virtually the same. Our English accents are also almost identical, as we were both brought up in the same suburb south of London. Someone once said they heard a very English voice at a carousel in an airport while collecting luggage and could have sworn it was me only to turn around and discover, indeed, that it was Julie Andrews!

Of course, I wanted to meet her and have a photo for total comparison. It seemed this would happen during rehearsals for the show surrounding AFI's Tribute to Robert Wise in 1998. Having directed her in *The Sound of Music*, it made perfect sense for Julie to be Mistress of Ceremonies for his special evening. So it was. At one point between rehearsals a couple of days prior to the actual telecast, one of the production guys had to collect her from the stage and take her back to the main part of the ballroom to speak with the producer. It was then that I was introduced to her. Julie was absolutely charming and seemed in no rush to disappear, but further conversation was not to be, and we only had time to say hello before she was whisked back on stage and said production guy, who had camera in hand at the ready, never did have an opportunity to take the picture. She did sign a poster for me, which still hangs in my living room, and yes, there was a very remote similarity in our physical appearance.

* * * * *

Still in the musical world on another occasion I met the legendary singer Eartha Kitt. Her most memorable songs included "*C'est si bon*" and at Christmas time every year "*Santa Baby*" would reappear. She was possibly most proud of Orson Welles statement when he called her "the most exciting woman in the world," and she was one of a kind, indeed.

In 1983 she made a documentary in which she starred as herself. Titled *All by Myself*, it told her life story and all the other characters in it were also played by themselves. The film premiered in Los Angeles on November 16, as a fundraising event for an organization called the Wright Institute. Its mission was to educate psychologists to practice at the highest level of professional competence; to analyze and evaluate research, theory, and practice; and to make appropriate lifelong use of the evolving body of psychological knowledge.

I had been retained to handle the premier but not being a very visible charity, let alone understanding exactly what they were trying to do, the evening was not a major financial success. Miss Kitt had agreed to do a Q&A session at the conclusion of the film. Although the audience was not overwhelming, interest was keen and the hope of increasing the badly needed funds was high. After everyone had taken their seats without any appearance from our star, the film began and I stood in the darkened lobby awaiting her arrival.

I only knew Eartha Kitt by reputation so I was a little apprehensive on two counts. To begin with, I wasn't at all sure she would turn up and even if she did, would she stay as planned for the

Q&A session after the screening? What would her mood be like? She wasn't known for being overly difficult, but she was no pushover, either, and I stood and waited as the minutes dragged by. I was dying for a glass of wine, but although the little bar in the foyer was open, complete with young man at the ready to pour whatever was called for, I thought that would look most unprofessional so I shifted from one foot to the other and continued to inspect my finger nails – "Should I have filed them?," I remember thinking – and waited.

Finally, some twenty minutes or so after the film had begun, her car pulled up and deposited her outside the theatre's entrance. It wasn't a particularly pleasant evening. A cold wind was blowing, so we both hurried inside and Miss Kitt looked anything but happy. She didn't apologize for being late but made a beeline for the bar calling out over her shoulder she hoped there was champagne available and it better be French, as anything else gave her a headache. Fortunately, the bartender was able to show her the label so she was satisfied. We both had a glass. I felt compelled to keep her company and welcomed her to the event, saying how appreciative everyone was and so looking forward to seeing her. After several swigs, things seemed to improve and she became quite chatty asking me various questions about my involvement with the Wright Institute and my role in the evening's proceedings.

A little later a rather worried looking Wright Institute executive appeared his expression turning to relief at the sight of the two ladies at the bar obviously indicating the guest of honor had arrived to fulfill her duties.

The evening proved a great success for those in attendance, and Eartha Kitt was a big hit after concluding a twenty-minute Q&A session followed by more champagne for all at the bar in the lobby. Despite the lack of financial gain, the Wright Institute was also delighted with the evening and the way it had been handled, so it certainly could be considered a *succès d'estime* at least.

Chapter Five:
Socializing In The 70's

The 1970s presented lots of opportunities for socializing with recognizable names! Like the time Jay Heifetz invited me to the Music Center to see P.D.Q. Bach. Jay was the youngest son of world-renowned violinist, Jascha Heifitz, and at the time was the head of marketing for the Los Angeles Philharmonic Orchestra and the Hollywood Bowl. It was early January 1974 and although I had never heard of P.D.Q. Bach, I soon learned such a concert was highly entertaining, very funny, and altogether lots of fun. I later discovered that the "P.D.Q." in Peter Schickele's world of parody while performing the works of the "only forgotten son" of Johann Sebastian Bach, stood for "pretty damn quick."

Another evening going to dinner with friends, we were joined by a new addition to the group in the form of actor Paul Sand. Paul had won a Tony Award in 1971 for his work on Broadway in *Paul Sills' Story Theatre*, in which he played eleven characters, including a dog! Now living above the famous carousel on Santa Monica Pier, his talents took him from theatre to film and television. He was a rather wild young man, but interesting and fun. After a lovely supper at the Konditori restaurant in Beverly Hills, we went to a screening of François Truffaut's new film *The Story of Adele H.* Revealing the life of the acclaimed French writer Victor Hugo's daughter Adèle, it told the tale of her obsessive but unrequited love for a military officer. It garnered its leading lady Isabelle Adjani a Best Actress nomination at the age of 20, making her the youngest such star ever to have received that honor.

* * * * *

I was often surprised to receive a phone call direct from the individual concerned, famous name or not, as happened on one occasion when I was at my desk working on AFI's Tribute Dinner for Bette Davis in 1977. Natalie Wood was on the other end of the line, and we had a lengthy conversation trying to work out how some of her friends could be organized to sit together for the event on March 1. This led to additional calls and further discussion with the likes of Julie Andrews and her husband, director Blake Edwards of *Pink Panther* and *Breakfast at Tiffany's* fame, Mia Farrow of television's *Peyton Place* and the film *Rosemary's Baby*, the English actress Juliet Mills from the television sitcom *Nanny and the Professor*, and finally the prolific composer and fellow Brit Leslie Bricusse, who had written a number of musicals, from *Doctor Doolittle* to *Willie Wonka & the Chocolate Factory*. They were all Natalie's friends, and by the time I got off the phone I felt I was one, too.

Paul Henreid came to one of the special events given at Greystone Mansion in those years. The terrace of this legendary mansion, built in the early 1900s, was the perfect spot for cocktails overlooking the gardens. On this occasion the current mayor of the city was in attendance for a special screening of Italian director Luchino Visconti's latest film, *The Innocent*. Paul Henreid had appeared in two timeless films by then, *Now, Voyager* with Bette Davis, in which he created one of cinema's most imitated scenes, lighting two cigarettes and slowly presenting one to her and perhaps, and even more memorably in his next role as Victor Laszlo, a heroic anti-Nazi leader in *Casablanca* with Humphrey Bogart and Ingrid Bergman. Henried came from a Trieste banking family that had been ennobled by the Habsburgs, so the story of romantic intrigue among the old world Italian aristocracy in *The Innocent* must have made him feel right at home. To sip a glass of wine with such a distinguished actor made for another rather intoxicating occasion.

One evening in late 1979, renowned director King Vidor used the Great Hall at Greystone to screen his latest film. It was a short documentary about the great painting legacy left by Andrew Wyeth titled *The Metaphor*. King was 85 years young then, and it seemed he would go on forever contributing to the film world as he had for some seven decades. He would tell stories of living in Beverly Hills at the turn of the last century, when Sunset Boulevard was lined with orange groves. One of his most acclaimed films, *The Champ*, had won him a Best Director Oscar. He went on to receive countless nominations for films like *War and Peace* (though he lost out to George Stevens for *Giant* on that occasion), but in 1979 he was honored by the Academy "for his incomparable achievements as a cinematic creator and innovator."

Another night that same year, I went to the Roxy, one of the most popular nightclubs on the Sunset Strip, to see a group called Tango, who were new to the A&M record label. Also on the bill was another group called Flash Cadillac, new clients at the Public Relations firm of my roommate Sue, so it was a double whammy of sorts. The highlight of the evening, however, should surely have been that we were sitting with Rick Springfield, a fact I didn't truly appreciate at all at the time, just commenting that he was very nice.

* * * * *

Some years later, I was able to attend some of the curricular activities for the Fellows attending the Conservatory, including lectures, seminars, screenings, and a variety of other programs. Given for the benefit of the students studying, occasionally there would be room for staff members. So it was on the occasion of Wednesday, March 17, 1976, that I was able to share the talk given by Anthony Hopkins, which proved to be a wonderful and insightful experience. He was very humble and extremely appreciative of his role in the film world, acknowledging that it was very much a "here today, gone tomorrow" existence. Little did he know that phrase would not apply to him, as he went on to an illustrious career winning many awards and proving his versatility many times over. Born and educated in Wales, Hopkins played a variety of characters on screen, from an English doctor in *The Elephant Man,* Prime Minister David Lloyd George in *Young Winston,* Captain Bligh in *Mutiny on the Bounty*, and perhaps his most famous role as Hannibal Lecter in *The Silence of the Lambs*. His numerous talents didn't exist in theatre and film alone -- he is also an accomplished composer and painter.

The year before it had been Robert Wise's turn to be a guest speaker, and he was such a sweet, gentle man that it seemed impossible that he would shout commands to his actors as the term "director" implies. Maybe he did and maybe he didn't, but one thing was for sure – he proved beyond a shadow of a doubt with *West Side Story* in 1961 and *The Sound of Music* in 1965 that he had no difficulty creating classics with seemingly effortless ease. His career in film had begun in spectacular fashion, too, when he was nominated for Best Film Editing for his work on Orson Welles's masterpiece *Citizen Kane.*

On another occasion, screenwriter Stewart Stern was featured. He gave a most impressive talk, which included discussion of the work for which he was most famous – writing the screenplay for *Rebel Without A Cause,* the second of James Dean's three highly memorable films. Back in the 50s, when it came out in England, I became an even more ardent fan and would never have thought I would meet anyone associated with him, let alone be his good friend! I was only fifteen when the movie was introduced in the UK, and it had an "X" certificate, which meant no one under the age of 16 was allowed in. The reason given for such a severe rating was the inclusion of a scene shot outside the Planetarium at Griffith Park Observatory when a fight ensues with the participants using switch-blade knives. I was not to be excluded, however, as I was dying to see it, having watched *East of Eden,* his first film, several times by then. I went with friends who had just had that all-important birthday so they bought tickets and went in, then scurried to one of the exits at the back of the theatre and let me in from an adjoining alley. In those days I never dreamt I would end up in Hollywood close to the Observatory, where to this day a plaque honoring James Dean stands prominently displayed at the entrance in Griffith Park.

When François Truffaut, the French director best known for *The 400 Blows,* was the seminar guest, the event was so popular that I not only failed to get in, but was stationed at the door with another employee to play security guard and throw out potential gatecrashers. A director, screenwriter, producer, actor, and film critic, Truffaut was also one of the founders of the French "New Wave," a group of French filmmakers of the 1950s and 1960s, who included Jean-Luc Godard, best known for *Breathless,* the story of a wandering criminal played by Jean-Paul Belmondo and his American girlfriend, Jean Seberg. Truffaut had also worked on this and, like *The 400 Blows,* it became an excellent example of the New Wave, encompassing new techniques like jump cuts and character asides. It was interesting to note the difference in appreciation between the general public, who were all gung ho about movie stars, as opposed to film students studying their craft. Obviously, M. Truffaut appealed to the latter.

Director John Schlesinger was another distinguished seminar guest. Arriving at the end of 1979, he had just completed *Yanks*. I was particularly interested in hearing what he had to say because of the English/American content not only of *Yanks,* but also of *Sunday Bloody Sunday,* which had been made a few years earlier. Set during World War II in Northern England, *Yanks* depicts the relationships between the brash American soldiers stationed in semi-rural England and the more reserved local women. By contrast, *Sunday Bloody Sunday* is about an unconventional love triangle and has absolutely no combat or fighting scenes.

One of the funniest and most memorable seminars was given by actor, comedian, filmmaker, composer, and songwriter Mel Brooks. His wife, the wonderful actress Anne Bancroft, came with him and was seated in the front row surrounded by students, all of whom quite probably identified with her best character, Mrs. Robinson in *The Graduate*, as she subtly defended herself and refused to admit, with a "would I lie to you?" smile, to seducing Dustin Hoffman! Anne had won an Academy Award for her leading role in *The Miracle Worker*, playing the tutor of Helen Keller. But on this occasion, the star was definitely Mel!

Mel wrote for television variety shows and eventually had his own series, *Get Smart*, which was built around the bumbling secret agents Maxwell Smart and Agent 99. The show ran for five years and paved Mel's way into the film world for hilarious farces like *The Producers*, *Blazing Saddles*, *Young Frankenstein*, *High Anxiety*, *History of the World Part I*, *Spaceballs*, and *Robin Hood: Men in Tights*.

With a perpetual smile, Mel spoke of his successes and failures, especially his initial failure to interest Anne Bancroft, whom he admitted to pursuing relentlessly until she had no option but to agree to a date. His persistence obviously paid off, and as with his entire career, he would never give up and the successes well outweighed the failures. He won innumerable awards, including an Emmy, Grammy, and Oscar (later he would win a Tony for a staged musical adaptation of *The Producers*) and seemed to be the epitome of success. At the conclusion of his talk, he invited everyone attending to a house-warming party later that month, and I was asked to put together a list for him. That led to one of the "Only in America" moments. It turned out to be a wonderful party and also in attendance were friends funny men Dom DeLuise and Carl Reiner, both regulars in Mel Brooks films, together with actress Hope Lange, best known at that time for her portrayal of Carolyn Muir in the television sitcom *The Ghost & Mrs. Muir*. One of the most memorable events of the evening came when the fountains in the pool were turned on, which could have been one of the reasons for the party! With just the click of a button each of the four corners erupted with a sky-high spout of water at the same time as floodlights illuminated the procedure. Years later, Caesar's Palace in Las Vegas would do the same thing, but on a much more sophisticated scale and its version would include classical music to complete the experience. For a private home however, this was very impressive to me and equally, very Hollywood and fell well and truly into my "Only in America" category!

* * * * *

In September 1977 I was given the responsibility of putting together a dinner party to be held in the foyer of Greystone Mansion, AFI's home base in Los Angeles, in honor of former Secretary of State Henry Kissinger, who had just left office.

Major movie studio mogul David Begelman and his wife Gladyce were listed on the invitation as hosts, with Mrs. Begelman heading the inevitable Ladies Committee in charge of logistics, which really meant flower arrangements. In fact, I didn't welcome this kind of assistance as, generally speaking, volunteers on such committees merely wanted the glory and congratulatory comments afterwards but were not prepared to do anything of any great significance to earn them. The contribution from Gladyce was short lived, as a big scandal involving Mr. Begelman's supposed studio embezzlement broke at that time and she subsequently disappeared. Many years later, in 1995, David Begelman would be found shot dead in a room at the Century Plaza Hotel in Los Angeles in an apparent suicide that many felt was due to his never really having recovered from the scandal.

Kissinger's dinner took place on the evening of Tuesday, October 11, 1977. His "date" was Angie Dickinson. Among the other celebrities assembled around tables of ten were Gregory and Veronique Peck, Henry and Shirlee Fonda, and Charlton and Lydia Heston. Director Hal Wallis was there, too, and I have to admit to harassing the poor man and asking innumerable questions about his association with Elvis Presley, which must have been very boring for him, but was wonderful for me. Mr. Wallis had been associated with so many classic films, including *Casablanca,* that I felt it was almost sacrilegious to talk about his Elvis movies – *G.I. Blues* and *Blue Hawaii* – in the same breath, but he was very gracious and pretended not to mind.

The entire evening was a major success in every way, and as people were leaving Charlton Heston kissed me on the cheek and offered his personal congratulations on a job well done.

Chapter Six:
The Exhausting, Exciting, and Educational 1980s

An important second phase of my life began to take root at the beginning of 1980. I was organizing all the special projects on a full-time basis for the American Film Institute but was quite often asked to handle events for other entities. Of course at that juncture I could not, but as time went on the idea of having my own business began to grow in my mind. The thought of being independent really began to appeal to me.

During the week before AFI's Life Achievement Award Tribute – in 1980 the honoree was James Stewart, – I moved my office to the Beverly Hilton Hotel. In those days of working full time for AFI, it proved to be much more convenient, and a better utilization of the days leading up to the event, to be on site and not have to waste time commuting back and forth. So it was, then, that on a Monday in February, I had phone conversations with participants in the show, technical people involved with lighting and sound, and the powers that be from AFI about seating the VIPs. Several people that day complimented me on my organizational skills and wondered how I could possibly keep calm with all the details and difficult situations faced on an hourly basis. You should do this for a variety of clients, they said, not just for one company, and be available to others. It was at midnight as I left the office when I started thinking seriously how that might be accomplished.

In retrospect, the 1970s formed the base for my financial future (I had bought my first house), and the 1980s liberated me from a 9-to-5 job! Being employed was very important – we all have to eat – but in the corporate world, especially for a woman, it was very difficult to make "real" money unless you made it big as a superstar or become a high-level studio executive.

That first year of the 1980s gave me time, a commodity I have cherished ever since. After I made the big decision to go out on my own and handle special events for more than one client, there were some lean months with little or no money coming in. But I had time -- a novelty to me -- to devote to whatever I felt inclined to do. One day running errands in the middle of the morning on a weekday, I marveled at the fact I could access a parking meter with no trouble at all! The traffic was light, I didn't have to be anywhere by a specific time, and I could relax and enjoy a whole new way of life.

This calm and contentment were very much tinged with worry, however, wondering where the next dollar was coming from. It was all fine and well to have a house, but with that came a mortgage, property taxes, and insurance, not to mention two dogs to feed and care for. So I had to be inventive and utilize the time available to me to good and profitable use while I awaited the multitude of new clients I hoped would arrive.

The first order of business was to find those new clients by letting everyone know I was available and ready to go to work.

I was very fortunate that even before relinquishing my desk at AFI, I was asked to continue handling the Life Achievement Award Tributes. At least I had one client and duly calendared the 1981 event to begin working in December 1980. This, however, was May, and the months between now and then had to be filled and had to produce income.

I had quite a number of enthusiastic supporters who agreed that someone like me in the party planning/event management business would be a great asset. One of them was *Hollywood Reporter* writer George Christy. His column, "The Great Life," covered all the social activities in Hollywood, including the Life Achievement Award Tribute every year. He had suffered the inevitable consequences of mismanaged events a number of times, and mine were not among them. At least I was assured of good press in at least one publication. In his column of March 9, 1982, he even included a photo of me with Irwin and Sheila Allen at the Frank Capra Tribute with the caption "with Jackie Frame, who masterfully coordinated the evening."

In readiness for my new career, I had business cards and letterhead printed and called myself "Event Management." On the back of the card it said, "Simply the Best," which was suggested to me by my designer friend Jack Schneider. I thought it rather chic. Too bad I didn't copyright it, as HBO uses it all the time, but I had it first! I installed an answering machine in my new home office and purchased an IBM Executive electric typewriter for the vast sum of $495. Duly armed with follow up material and no excuse for missed messages, I began to seek out projects.

I ran into a lot of situations where "talk is cheap" fit the bill, and Hollywood is not known as the most honest or sincere place in the world, so I took the rough with the smooth and as a colleague succinctly put it one day, "Everyone says 'let me know how I can help' - you do and they don't!" Get used to it!

I must say I got "P" for "perseverance," for I made use of all the contacts and connections I had in my endeavors to handle parties or premiers, fundraisers or conventions, weddings, bar mitzvahs - you name it I'd do it! So many people were enthusiastic about my decision that I felt something must come from somewhere. And of course eventually it did.

My first lucky break came in August when a business associate, Pat Ryan, suggested I phone a man named Clive David with whom she had done some event planning business in the past. Mr. David was a highly successful and well-recognized event planner, not to be confused with music mogul Clive Davis, and I was thrilled at the prospect of meeting him. We agreed that I would go to his home office at five o'clock the following afternoon. When he answered the door his first words were "Hello, I'm Clive David. I'm gay, Jewish and honest. Do come in." We had a wonderful first meeting culminating in dinner at Hymies Fish Market in Beverly Hills. It was evident right from the start we would get along, and in fact he asked me there and then to work on his next big project: "A Tribute to Men and Women of Achievement" to celebrate "The Bicentennial of the City of Los Angeles," to be held on Saturday, April 25, 1981.

Even though the Bicentennial wasn't taking place until April, there was a lot of preliminary work to be done, which meant that Clive and I would be in constant touch on the phone every day. This event was to be First Class all the way, with a white-tie ball and gala performance to take place at Metromedia Square in Hollywood.

One afternoon, while making calls to potential guests who would be honored as well as take part in the Gala, I got a charming refusal from

Danny Kaye who said he would have loved to come but refused to wear white-tie.

We had a large contingent of volunteers to help handle the presentations of medals and certificates of appreciation to all the "Men and Women of Achievement." Each personality would receive individual attention with instructions as to where to be and at what time and so on. This necessitated a large number of rehearsals with stand-ins for the celebrities, and we spent frequent evenings at Metromedia coordinating all of that. Clive was the genius behind the whole thing and left no stone unturned. From contacting those to be honored and those performing in the show, he arranged for the design and printing of the invitations, the program book, the medals, the certificates, the color scheme for the linens at dinner, flower arrangements, menus, donated wines and spirits, city permits, sponsors, and so on. My most important responsibility was to organize the seating and guest lists. That alone proved to be one of the most challenging tasks of any event and one, which Clive, by his own admission, just did not want to deal with and was very happy to pass on to someone else.

The evening of Saturday, April 25, 1981 was a truly memorable and historic event. Just about everyone who was anyone attended including then Mayor of the City, Tom Bradley.

There were to be 200 "achievers" present, a cross section of "those men and women whose endeavors make the City outstanding" was how the program book put it. Together with the illustrious group of citizens, a glittering array of local talent was invited to be part of the show, which later would become a television special. Joining Frank Sinatra, legendary actresses Greer Garson and Lillian Gish were joined by Gregory Peck, Shirley MacLaine, and Natalie Wood. Comedians

Steve Allen and Sid Caesar shared the stage with television personality Merv Griffin and piano man Liberace, while Rosemary Clooney, Carol Lawrence, and Dionne Warwick voiced their talent in song.

There were the inevitable situations in which guests who had not responded or, worse, had sent their regrets, but in fact showed up and we had to find somewhere for them to sit, but that's when I learned about Plans B, C, and D!

The evening proved to be an unqualified success and became the start of a wonderful working relationship for me with Clive covering momentous future events.

* * * * *

During the lean months at the beginning of my independent lifestyle, I realized that I would have to find alternative ways to generate income so I got a real estate license and continued my association with the celebrity world by either showing or selling them houses.

Wearing my real estate agent hat, there was an inevitable overlap that became evident when I showed a young actress named Elizabeth Pena what would become her first house. It was in Silver Lake, a somewhat trendy neighborhood east of Hollywood quite close to downtown Los Angeles. In those days it was "up and coming," and Pena was very excited at the prospect of owning her own home. Coming off a thirteen-week run of a television comedy series called *I Married Dora*, she had very smartly decided this was a good investment. I seem to remember she paid about $275,000. She never did become a big star, but I remember her as delightful, bubbly, and fun! Her house in 2010 would have appreciated to at least $1,275,000.

Another celebrity couple to whom I showed property were Miguel Ferrer, the oldest of José Ferrer's five children (Dad probably best remembered for his role in *Cyrano* on both stage and screen), and first woman television news anchor Kelly Lange's daughter, also named Kelly. The couple was engaged at the time and looking for a house in Laurel Canyon. They didn't stay engaged and never did buy anything, at least not from me, but it was nice to know them, albeit somewhat briefly.

Then one afternoon Jenny Agutter, an English actress who had starred in the BBC television series *The Railway Children* and then in the film of the same name back in the 1960s, called looking to buy a house. I remember thinking it strange that celebrities would call a real estate office just like ordinary people, and then realized of course that they are just the same as everyone else. Jenny was one of the few child stars to go on to an illustrious film career covering many decades. Continuing that trend in 2012, she joined the cast of the popular BBC television drama *Call the Midwife*.

During those days, I also showed the old Betty Hutton estate on Hollyridge Drive in the Hollywood Hills, as well as the home of actor Pierce Brosnan, who would go on to play James Bond in four films. He lived in a very pretty multitiered home with a most interesting pool tucked away in a rock formation on the side of the house. It was just too bad he was never there at the same time as I was.

On another occasion, together with other agents, we looked at Rudy Vallee's estate when it came on the market and I was reminded of a party I had attended there several years earlier when he was in residence. I remember being so impressed by the hallway leading from the front door into the main part of the house where a street sign stated the name as being "Rue de Vallee." It was still there in 1988, and the house was listed at $4.4 million.

According to public records, Barbara Stanwyck had once owned a house on a street called Hollymount in the Cahuenga Pass area of Hollywood, which we viewed as a possible listing on one occasion. It was supposedly going to sell for close to a million dollars, but as it was equally close to the Hollywood Freeway, I had my doubts about that one. We didn't get the listing anyway.

Added to all this activity, I continued working with AFI on the annual Life Achievement Award Tributes as well as other smaller gatherings and seemed to be constantly on the go.

* * * * *

My main focus in the early months of the year was always on AFI, and in 1981 the honoree for the Life Achievement Award was one of my all-time favorites, Fred Astaire. I was reminded of my personal encounter with Mr. Astaire a few years earlier, when he attended the 1976 Tribute to director William Wyler. On that occasion, at a production meeting when the logistics of getting the celebrities to and from the celebrations came up, Astaire was on the list. One of several VIP guests was First Lady Betty Ford, and as the President was not able to accompany her, an escort had to be provided. Fred Astaire had been asked to fill the role, which he acknowledged he would be delighted to do. It then remained for someone to collect Mr. Astaire from his home and accompany him to the Beverly Wilshire Hotel where Mrs. Ford was staying so that they could proceed to the festivities and arrive together.

I don't think I have ever responded to anything as fast as when I volunteered for that assignment! What made it even better was that everyone thought it was a very praiseworthy gesture on my part, as I would be extremely busy at the time with inevitable last-minute activities and traumas leading up to the big night. Needless to say, I wouldn't have missed it for the world.

I remember very clearly sitting in the back of the limo going up Benedict Canyon to the Astaire residence and ringing the bell with Fred himself answering the door with an irritated greeting, "You're late!" Indeed, I was late but I had a good reason, and had it been in the days of cell phones I would have called to let him know. It seemed Mrs. Ford was running late and we had been instructed to get to the Beverly Wilshire Hotel at least thirty minutes later than originally planned. Rather than bore poor Fred with my company for a full half hour, I arrived ten minutes late so that he would only have twenty minutes to kill before continuing. I must say I've never been so charmingly "told off" to this day! He wasn't really cross, just nervous that he would be late, I think, and after a few pleasantries as to who I was and what role I played in the evening's festivities, I asked him if he himself had a favorite film. "Mine or somebody else's?," he asked. "Either," I replied to which he said as far as his own movies were concerned he never thought about the past, never watched any, just concentrated on the now and the future. So what was in the future? He said there were a few irons in the fire but nothing he could really talk about yet. He didn't want to tempt fate with regard to something he really would like to happen by discussing it only to have all concerned disappointed if it didn't work out. I couldn't resist telling him how much I had enjoyed everything he had ever done, in fact the very first film I ever saw was *Easter Parade*, in which he "walked down the Avenue" with Judy Garland. I reminisced how my cousin and I had watched spellbound as he and Ginger Rogers danced their way in and out of classics like *Top Hat, Flying Down to Rio, Blue Skies, Shall We Dance,* and *Swing Time,* among others. But as he had said he didn't want to dwell anywhere but in the now, that was enough nostalgia, so we then talked about cooking, gardening, and other more mundane practices. All too soon, it was time to leave.

We drove to the Beverly Wilshire, and I took him up to Mrs. Ford's suite where two very burly security guards were guarding her door. They whisked Fred through, and I was sent packing.

Betty Ford was an ardent admirer of Fred Astaire and she spoke briefly from her seat at the head table, saying how much she admired Mr. Wyler's work and had so enjoyed his movies, but in a change of celebrity status she went on to say one of her fondest film related memories had been at a White House dinner where she had so enjoyed "dancing across (she pronounced it 'accraust') the floor" with the legendary Mr. Astaire.

At the end of the evening, I collected Fred from where he had been abandoned at the head table after the secret service had whisked off his "date" to her waiting limo. To his intense relief, as he really had no idea in which direction to turn, I took him by the hand and led him through all the fans in the lobby to his own limo waiting to take him home. He was most appreciative of being taken care of even though we were nearly blinded by a huge presence of flashing press corps taking photos for their respective publications. Despite the number that must have been taken, regrettably I could never track one down. It remains however, an evening I will never forget. And I think I was forgiven for my tardy arrival.

I was really excited at the prospect of being involved with Fred's very own tribute, listening to the stories from his co-stars and friends and watching all the wonderful film clips I remembered so well from my youth!

I wasn't disappointed at all as it was a fabulous evening attended by the film industry's finest, especially in the dance category. Mikhail Baryshnikov and Gene Kelly were there, as were the great choreographers Bob Fosse and Hermes Pan. Charlton Heston was the host and David Niven Master of Ceremonies. Among the other admirers were legends like Jack Benny, George Burns, James Cagney, and Pulitzer Prize winning journalist Art Buchwald, as well as Fred's most famous dance partners. Eleanor Powell, who had starred in *Broadway Melody of 1940* and tapped her way into the history books with "Begin the Beguine," could be seen sitting at a table next to that of Cyd Charisse, who appeared with Fred in *The Band Wagon* and *Silk Stockings*. Audrey Hepburn, who had made her dancing debut with Fred in the musical film *Funny Face*, recalled how her "feet turned into great lumps of lead" the first time she rehearsed a routine with him. Barbra Streisand, Dory Previn, Bernadette Peters, Sammy Cahn, and Neil Diamond rounded out the music section, but noticeably absent was Ginger Rogers and all kinds of gossip floated round about that. She sent a letter, which Fred read during his acceptance speech and although he was kind, it didn't sound very sincere.

* * * * *

The beginning of the year became doubly encouraging when I was asked to work on an event taking place in New York on May 11, 1981, to commemorate the 33rd birthday of the State of Israel. Named "Celebration 33," there was to be a special screening of a new film called *The Chosen* in honor of the event. Starring Maximilian Schell and Rod Steiger, it told the story of an unlikely friendship between two teenage Jewish boys from different sects living in Brooklyn towards the end of World War II.

I felt like the classic successful businesswoman as I boarded the TWA flight and took a cab to the New York Sheraton on my first all-expense paid trip. It was exciting the following day to attend a meeting at Carnegie Hall, where clips of the film were shown. I met Robby Benson, who played one of the boys in the film, and Ely and Edie Landau, who produced it. Robby had appeared in several earlier films, but never with a co-starring major role, and he was very excited. Jeremy Kagan, a former AFI Fellow, was the director, so it was a bit like old home week! Jewish comedian and satirist Alan King, well known for his biting wit, introduced everyone and handled the press conference later in the day. I found the entire experience stimulating and exciting.

This event, which in fact never did come off, although the film was released later in the year, was planned on a very grand scale with representatives from cities all over the country flown in to participate in the early stages so that they could take back details and information to promote the event in their own states. The ambitious aim was to raise fifty million dollars in one night from the proceeds of the film when it was shown in theatres throughout the land.

A gentleman named Haim Bernstein seemed to be in charge, and an incredibly rich businessman named Meshulam Riklis was the moneyman behind the event. I remember him commenting at one point that it didn't really matter how much money was lost on promotion because he would still be able to eat breakfast the next morning. That would prove to be just as well based on the negative response that was to follow.

However, not knowing that at the time once back in Los Angeles, I worked very hard to put a Women's Committee together and got absolutely nowhere. It seemed that everyone was too busy, unavailable, didn't know enough about it, didn't have the time or inclination to find out, or just weren't interested right off the bat! Truth to tell, they were all spread too thin with other charitable works to fit another one in, especially if it was to benefit an "out of town" charity. I did get a meeting with the Israeli Consulate, but that didn't go anywhere although it proved a memorable experience as to gain access to the offices I had to go through complicated security checks and show my identification through a bullet-proof glass window. It had never occurred to me I could be in a potentially dangerous situation.

In a desperate effort to drum up interest and attendance, I was told to plan a party in Los Angeles and invite as many movers and shakers as could be found. Coming in from New York would be Meshulam Riklis, Rod Steiger, and Robby Benson, the stars of the film, the producers Ely and Edie Landau, and from LA the Israeli Consul General himself, Benjamin Navon. Response was poor despite the fact everything was offered on a complimentary basis. After repeated requests to find at least 200 guests, we only managed to gather about 100 and they were pretty much fillers who wanted a free meal and a glass of wine.

A lot of money was lost. The event never did take place so I only got part of my fee, but presumably Mr. and Mrs. Riklis (he was married to actress Pia Zadora at that time) continued enjoying their breakfasts and I chalked it up as a most interesting experience.

* * * * *

There was always a lot of talk about potential events, and I had to get used to the initial excitement being overtaken by disappointment when nine out of ten projects fell through.

One other such occasion was for a place called Sojourn House. I was approached to help with a fundraiser it had planned to continue efforts to "provide alcohol and other drug treatments to those in need." In addition, they offered counseling services to adolescents, adults and their families. It was a very good cause, and Alan Alda had been set to host the party on the set of *M*A*S*H*. Attractive as that sounded, it didn't get off the ground. As I was to learn over the years, this type of "cause" just didn't appeal to enough people who could afford to buy tickets. Terminally ill children and other health issues seemed to get the best response.

On another occasion I met with a man called Morton Sunshine, who was the executive director of Variety Clubs International and handled a huge number of fundraising activities for them on both the east and west coasts. Although we kept in touch over the years, regrettably nothing came of that either.

Another "no go" for me at least was for the 1984 LA Olympics. I had various meetings with those in charge but there was no niche for my services as a professional who would charge a fee. They were going to rely heavily on volunteers, which was a shame as I think it would have been fun. However, at that stage I was not in a position to do volunteer work.

A friend who worked for HBO told me the network were planning a big 10th Anniversary party, and we got all excited about the potential for that. However, they encountered various budgetary problems and it became another project to bite the dust as far as I was concerned.

A very welcome call from my friend and former associate party planner extraordinaire, Clive David, came in July asking me to think about working on a party connected with the famous Beverly Hills shopping promenade, Rodeo Drive. A new addition called the Rodeo Collection was planned and would have a grand opening within the next few years. He was planning on being the organizer. I kept my fingers crossed on that one. Scheduled for June, various meetings took place and I started thinking quite positive about it. However the opening date was pushed back and then postponed indefinitely, so my enthusiasm began to dwindle.

One day I met with Trevor Valentine from the American-British Chamber of Commerce. Although I never handled any of its events, that led to a membership involvement where I met some wonderfully interesting people to remind me of home. At their Christmas party, where *My Fair Lady's* Rex Harrison was the guest of honor, I was mixing and mingling with the likes of Michael York, Hermione Gingold (so wonderfully English in *Gigi* singing "I Remember It Well" with Maurice Chevalier), and publicist Jerry Pam, who represented Michael Caine and Roger Moore.

But even with two hefty projects for 1981, I still needed something to tide me over so as well as continuing to look for new projects I started a small garden business and had weekend plant sales in my driveway. This led to some holiday business, especially at Christmas, as I specialized in delivering orders to homes or offices. It also afforded me the opportunity to meet my neighbors.

Being in Hollywood, some of those neighbors were actors. Dee Wallace and Christopher Stone lived just down the road from me on Ivarene Avenue. They had just finished a movie together – a horror classic called *The Howling* – and came to my very first plant sale. From then on not only did they become my best customers, but also great friends. Eventually I did the flowers for their wedding as well as designing and planting the patio of their house from where they would be married. I don't remember a couple more crazy about each other as those two. Although they would work together on several movie projects and Dee would go on to a very successful acting career, her most visible role probably as Drew Barrymore's mother in Steven Spielberg's immortal *E.T. The Extra-Terrestrial*, but their happiness would be short lived. Chris died of a heart attack in 1995. But they had some happy family life, and a daughter, Gabrielle, was born in 1988. I lost touch with them, but during the time we were neighbors I saw them often and even spent Thanksgiving Dinner at their new house in Woodland Hills a couple of times, on one occasion meeting Dee's 94-year-old grannie. To give you an idea how devoted Chris was, I remember at one of my plant sales he bought Dee a beautiful cut flower arrangement which he took home and presented to her and then twenty minutes later they left on a trip.

* * * * *

1981 became a year of ups and downs to put it mildly. I suppose being in business on my own for the first time I should have expected a somewhat uncertain period of time, which indeed it proved to be.

On one occasion I met with delightful people from a place called the Poison Center, who were all gung ho to put on a fundraising "something" (that was up to me) to generate funds for their cause. It was difficult to explain that although immensely worthy, their endeavors weren't very high on the sympathy list and that it would be difficult to make any money. Most companies who wanted to put on events could only see the potential incoming funds and forgot the outgoing expenses before breaking even, let alone generating anything financially positive.

Chapter Six

Sometimes ideas from well-intentioned people led to a monumental waste of time either in person (which was very difficult to get away from) or the phone, which could be equally tricky. But I began to get quite adept at figuring out ways and means of escape. When a particularly wordy gentleman had me on the phone for over an hour (and not for the first time), he went on his way in a matter of seconds when I announced I was instigating a new consultation fee for commitments over a certain length of time.

* * * * *

Towards the end of 1981, things slowed to a crawl. It got so bad I hired on with a temporary secretarial agency and was sent out at $9 an hour to play typist again. I had to bite the bullet, swallow my pride, and not treat this as a defeat. The only way I could do that was to pretend it was a role in a film and make-believe I was someone else. In fact, the two firms I worked for saw right through me quite soon and realized I wasn't just an "ordinary" temp. I took this as a great compliment and in the end I was asked to take of care of their special projects and events. I was just a born organizer. Not only did I have to suffer this setback in my new career, but had to get up at crack of dawn as the hours were 8 to 5. I never was any good at getting up in the morning and years later when I was back in control, I would write late starting times into my contracts.

* * * * *

During my stint at AFI, I had become known for my efficient handling of phone calls. The switchboard would get enquiries about film and television in the US from all over the world and if they didn't know where to send them, I would get the call. I found it fascinating trying to come up with the answers, but what I became famous for was getting back to people even if I didn't have the answers. They were so appreciative of a call back regardless of whether I had any information that it gave me a great opportunity to establish a rapport with any number of foreign entities.

One such caller was a chap named Jerry Downing, who hailed from Brisbane, Australia, and had a production company specializing in documentaries for television. So it was that in September of this rather disappointing year a ray of hope glimmered in the form of RWB Productions.

Jerry and his crew were in the planning stages of a program to be shot all over the world titled *Who Stole My Childhood*. In today's world, the internet provides much more transparency, but back then you didn't hear much about child prostitution, abuse and neglect, incestuous relationships, and so on. It was an ambitious piece and they wanted me to do the on-camera interviews (they liked the sound of an English accent), which of course I agreed to do. The entire project was not without its traumas, however, which began from the very start.

The four-man crew arrived in Los Angeles and straight off the plane attempted to take a cab, only to be overtaken by the LAPD, with guns drawn, the driver arrested and taken away while they looked on in consternation. It was explained to them they had had a lucky escape, as apparently there was a scam afoot at the time where passengers were being abducted and robbed at gunpoint. In all likelihood they would all have been killed and their cash and equipment stolen one officer told them. Welcome to LA!

Extensive research was needed, and one of the first programs was a lecture given by an LAPD officer named Lloyd Martin, who talked about child abuse. He spoke at a school in a place in East Los Angeles called Diamond Bar, and his primary focus was to explain precisely what a pedophile/child molester was. The definition for *pedophilia* comes from two Greek words meaning "child" and "friendly love" or "friendship." Inspector Martin emphasized the difference between a *pedophile* and a *child molester*, noting that they were not necessarily one and the same. Pedophilia, he said, was a psychiatric disorder that caused an adult or older adolescent to experience a primary or exclusive sexual attraction to prepubescent children. However, unlike a child molester, who tended to force undesired sexual behavior on a passive individual, a pedophile usually took his time and developed a relationship that led in the same direction but without necessarily using force. He stressed how important it was that the term pedophile not be bandied about to cover everyone involved with child abuse. He was not defending pedophiles, just trying to explain the difference.

Pedophiles, he went on, were generally only interested in children between certain ages and once out of that range, interest was lost. An example of how far a pedophile would go to achieve his goal could include marrying a woman with a child, or children, in a specific age range, so that access via recreational activities like hunting trips, church, being driven to school, and so on would be very easy to come by. Here again, Martin stated that the relationship was usually built very gradually and didn't always end with a sex act at all (although most of the time it did) which made people think it was a child abuser at work.

Our first interview took place in Encino in the San Fernando Valley with Parents Anonymous. Founded in 1969, the organization was dedicated to preventing child abuse and neglect and creating a community of happy and productive family life. This was followed by a visit to the California Lutheran College and an interview with Michael Agopian, who would later go on to write articles on child abduction and sex offenders. More information on our subject was forthcoming here with the observation that consumption of child pornography could be an indicator of a pedophile but not necessarily a child molester. Apparently, pedophilia was first formally recognized in the late 19th century, when a significant amount of research in the area led to documentation indicating that men seem to be most prone to the condition, though there are also women who exhibit the disorder. We were told that there is no cure for pedophilia but that there are therapies that can reduce child sexual abuse. No one seems to know what causes the condition, though some studies of pedophilia in child sex offenders have correlated it with various neurological abnormalities and psychological pathologies. At times it all got a bit too technical for me as we became privy to information and facts that were difficult to listen to, and even harder to accept, but nonetheless horrifying in a time where none of this was really discussed.

    In San Diego, south of LA we taped interviews with members of the San Diego Police Department and the Children's Hospital and Health Care Center before heading across the country to venues in New York. The East Coast was extremely cold, and the day I flew in, a raging blizzard greeted me. Just one bus was left at JFK Airport to deliver the remaining passengers to a subway station. All the cab drivers had gone home, and, after us, no more flights were allowed to land so we were grateful for anything on wheels. I had been told that under no circumstances should I travel alone on the subway, especially after dark, but the circumstances being what they were, I didn't have much choice. Off I went with the group, and not being on my own, I felt it was OK. The train took us to the center of the city and after that it was a very short cab ride to the Barbizon Plaza, where I was staying. I remember a young woman sitting opposite me who had flip-flops on (it wasn't cold in LA and certainly not snowing) and obviously she hadn't checked the weather forecast before boarding the flight. The snow was 6" thick in the center of Manhattan, and even a short walk such as that from the cab up the steps into the lobby of the hotel would have been most uncomfortable for her. I was freezing and I had boots on.

One of the most colorful figures we would meet in New York was a Dr. Judianne Densen-Gerber. In 1966, she founded Odyssey House, a drug-free therapeutic community helping addicts recover. Then she extended her influence into areas like child pornography, which was what we talked about in her interview. She was one of a kind and totally dedicated to her cause. With her bouffant hairdo and rhinestone-studded glasses, she was quite a character. When she set her mind to something, she would invariably get her way, as she did after picketing in front of Governor Nelson Rockefeller's house to demand funds for her program. They eventually became good friends and she got what she wanted.

On one occasion I had to interview a couple still together after the father had had an incestuous relationship with his daughter. The mother knew about it. To me, that was an impossible situation but it seemed the wife couldn't entertain the thought of losing her husband under any circumstances. I remember sitting in shock and being very thankful I had a script to refer to, as I was speechless.

Yet another example of deceit in such circumstances came from one of three sisters who had suffered at the hands of her father, who had promised her that he wouldn't touch the other two sisters if she didn't give him away. Of course, he was molesting all three with the same story, and they didn't discover his treachery until all were in their twenties.

On several occasions during additional interviews unbelievable facts would be revealed by medical personnel, doctors, child psychiatrists, and the like. One such revelation told us about factories in foreign countries that manufactured instruments to enlarge the various anatomy of small children, even babies, to accommodate perverse adults.

We asked Christina Crawford, the daughter of actress Joan, if she would host the program. She was the perfect choice, being the writer of *Momie Dearest*, an autobiographical account of alleged child abuse by her mother Joan.

The crew went on to shoot scenes in San Francisco and other parts of the US, as well as overseas in Yugoslavia, but in the end the finished film never made it to the small screen, at least not to American audiences. Finally, at the very end of the year I could sink my teeth into the next major project for AFI, their Tribute to director John Huston to be held in March the following year.

* * * * *

John Huston's films are legendary and considered classics. He is almost as famous for his multi talented daughter Angelica. To maintain his image, we wanted to come up with something really special to make the evening a truly memorable event and we did.

Someone found the original *Maltese Falcon* statuette from John's famous film of the same name stashed and abandoned at the back of a sound stage. We had a mold made and on each table for desert that evening, a chocolate Maltese Falcon sat center stage. Some chocoholic guests couldn't resist and broke it down, but several drew lots as to who would take it home intact. I think that was one of the most spectacular conclusions to a dinner we ever had.

Several years later in 1987, Mr. Huston was invited to attend the Tribute to Barbara Stanwyck. By then aged 80, he was wheel chair bound and was pushed by daughter Angelica. Gracious as ever, he charmed everyone quite possibly because by then age had mellowed him and his face was creased with laugh lines. I don't know who garnered more attention – father or daughter!

* * * * *

As 1983 got underway, business started picking up and in the Spring I was introduced to David Hinkley, the Western Region Director of Amnesty International. Amnesty was interested in putting on fundraisers later in the year, so we started scouting locations. Eventually, it was decided to use the London Club in Los Angeles for the first one on April 8. Although it wasn't a massive financial success, raising only about $30,000, it was a wonderful publicity vehicle and got the group lots of press coverage thanks to the celebrity guests, who included Meryl Streep, Walter Matthau, Richard Widmark, Beatrice Straight (whose claim to fame was her role in the 1976 film *Network*, where she was on screen for five minutes and forty seconds, making that the shortest performance ever to win an Academy Award), Susan Blakeley, best known for her leading role in the television miniseries *Rich Man, Poor Man*, and Terri Garr, whose appearance in Mel Brooks *Young Frankenstein* had been unforgettable

Amnesty pressed on, though, and it was decided the next event would take place at a restaurant in Hollywood named Dar Maghreb. Famous for its Moroccan décor and authentic cuisine, most of the dishes were finger food eaten while reclining amidst massive pillows on low-slung couches or the floor! Belly dancers completed the entertainment and atmospheric experience.

Amnesty's night there was memorable indeed, but without the Belly dancers! The special guest, Dr. Hang Ngor, gave an incredibly moving speech detailing his horrific experiences in Cambodia, from which it seemed miraculous that he was alive at all. Eventually getting himself to the US, it seemed ironic somehow that he would win an Academy Award for portraying himself in the movie *The Killing Fields* and ultimately talk about it in Hollywood. Also contributing to the evening's content were Steve Allen, Malcolm McDowell, and Mary Steenburgen, always staunch supporters of this particular cause and again, although not a massive financial success, it drew much needed attention to the organization.

The restaurant had become a landmark by then, despite its particularly unpleasant owner and I often wonder if he was part of the reason it closed. It was always such a shame when working conditions were tarnished by rude and difficult personalities. It was totally unproductive, too, but those involved never seemed to realize it.

One of Amnesty International's most successful ventures took place on the evening of Monday, September 15, 1986, at the Beverly Hilton Hotel in Beverly Hills. By then I was so familiar with the Beverly Hilton (because AFI's Life Achievement Award had been held there for so many years) that it was like coming home. It's always great to work with people whom you know and can rely upon, and such was the case on this occasion. Everything went right, and the celebrity input was first rate. Master of the keyboard Dudley Moore was hysterical, and I was reminded of the night in London at the Fortune theatre when I was twenty and laughing just as hard then at the antics in *Beyond the Fringe*. Here we were 24 years later, and still falling about! Also lending support were Amanda McBroom, who had written the immortal song "The

Rose," made famous by Bette Midler who sang it in the film of the same name, and Billy Davis another songwriter whose claim to fame was his composition for Coca-Cola "I'd Like to Teach the World to Sing (In Perfect Harmony)." Included with the musical personalities was Kris Kristofferson, a multi-talented and somewhat overlooked personality, who was perhaps best known for writing and recording such hits as "Me and Bobby McGee," and "Help Me Make It Through The Night." Rounding out the group was comedian Bill Erwin, better known as a clown but also an outstanding character actor from film and television who would go on to win an Emmy nomination for appearances on *Seinfeld* in later years.

* * * * *

Then I was told by a friend in New York to call a man named James Lazarus in Florida, the current President of the Young Presidents Organization. To qualify for membership in the YPO, a person had to have become president or chairman of a multi million-dollar corporation employing at least fifty people before the age of forty. Obviously, such an organization did not need to raise funds for itself, but it did want to organize a conference for all their members. La Costa Resort in North San Diego County, California had been chosen as their destination.

Before the conference, I went down to La Costa Resort several times for meetings with the staff and media people who would be involved, as all the sessions would be taped. There were also social activities to plan, one of which was to be a shopping spree at Neiman Marcus for the wives while their successful CEO husbands were discussing high finance, at least in part to continue providing the funds for such exotic shopping sprees. I was not very familiar with this particular department store as it was way out of my price range, but it certainly made for a pleasant meeting. Too bad they weren't giving away any samples.

Of course, there would be a lot of paperwork to assemble and put in three-ring binders covering each day, together with name badges and all the other paraphernalia that goes with a conference.

I always enjoyed the social fringe benefits that went with these assignments, and this was no exception as Jim and Ellie Lazarus held a cocktail party in their suite on my first visit for all the additional employees who would be involved. This included personnel from the travel agency and local press, together with the likes of my staff and me, who would be handling the administrative logistics. After that they went on to host a marvelous dinner at a local restaurant and I remember marveling, "This is work?"

The actual conference opened with guest registration. This gave me a wonderful opportunity to observe the difference between the West and East coast attendees. The most snooty and unpleasant were the wives from the East coast.

On the first evening, there was a Mexican Carnival by the pool, complete with mariachi music and piñatas, margaritas, and a groaning buffet of chile rellenos, tacos, tortillas, and all the trimmings. It was a lovely festive start on a beautiful, balmy night under the stars.

Opening ceremonies began the following morning, with guest speakers and a lunch before an evening concert that we called "Symphony on the Green." It involved a picnic on a grassy hill above La Costa with everyone supplied with blankets and a basket of goodies filled with wine and champagne. This was followed by fireworks and revelry, providing a fitting end to the first day.

Chapter Six

The next day will remain in my mind forever. A demonstration of the Mac computer as part of the conference program gave me an opportunity to operate the famous "mouse" and learn more about Apple's technology. Fighting with DOS on a PC, I knew from the very first moment that this was for me. I found it utterly fascinating and from then on decided as soon as I was back in my office that it would be a thoroughly justified addition.

A special screening had been arranged that night after dinner. The movie was *All The Right Moves*, starring Tom Cruise. This particular vehicle was presumably chosen because all those viewing it had done just that, hence their membership in the YPO! A studio executive named Jerry Bergman handled a Q&A session afterwards and despite a delayed start time, everyone thoroughly enjoyed it.

The breakfast speaker the next morning was a woman named Toni Grant, a psychologist and radio host. A pioneer in the advice-giving genre, she was one of the first to have her own talk show. She gave a most interesting discourse, though I did wonder if the audience would have liked something a little juicier as she had become famous for not mincing her words.

After another very full day, a spectacular evening concluded the proceedings at Fairbanks Ranch Country Club, a gorgeous facility in the exclusive area of Rancho Santa Fe, just a few miles from La Costa. Fittingly, it was a black-tie affair starting with cocktails on one tennis court, followed by dinner on another, and then dancing in the Club House. Everywhere was decorated with beautiful floral arrangements and blossoms from floor to ceiling.

It was a truly remarkable few days for all those participating. Despite the long hours and exhausting schedule, it proved to be one of the most memorable events I ever handled.

* * * * *

Although Los Angeles was a comparatively young city without huge historical significance, there were any number of "mature" buildings from classic Victorian era houses, 1920s California bungalows, and places like Union Station and the Bradbury Building, among others, proving there should be a Conservancy Society, which there was.

That was when I started to work on a fundraising project to aid in the restoration of the Ennis-Brown house in the Los Feliz area of Los Angeles.

Located in the hills north of downtown and close to another famous landmark, the Greek Theatre, the Ennis-Brown house was designed by Frank Lloyd Wright in 1923 for Charles and Mabel Ennis. It represented the fourth and largest of Wright's textile block designs and was constructed primarily of pre-cast concrete blocks. It is said the design was based on ancient Mayan temples. Although it looked literally "solid as a rock," it turned out not to be so. Even before it was completed, some of the concrete blocks had cracked and sections of the walls buckled under the strain of so much weight.

Eric Wright, the architect's grandson, worried about the house falling into more disrepair as time went on and needed ideas for a fundraiser to replace the crumbling bricks of a massive retaining wall holding up the hill at the side of the house.

Here again, bricks and mortar are not a sympathetic charity, so we had to try and think of something a little bit different to pull in funds! It was decided to call it a "Block Party" and instead of just asking for money, we would sell individual blocks, which actually meant bricks, although anyone who has ever seen a Frank Lloyd Wright house knows that is not a small red clay number, but more like a mini boulder of thick grey granite. Eventually we sold about fifty, albeit with a struggle.

Another famous grandchild of Mr. Wright was actress Anne Baxter. She had starred in a number of films and won the Academy Award for Best Supporting Actress in 1946 for *The Razor's Edge*. Her most famous film was *All About Eve*, which starred Bette Davis. Add to that appearing in Orson Welles's *The Magnificent Ambersons* as well as *The Ten Commandments* with Charlton Heston and Yul Brynner, and you have a very impressive repertoire.

Miss Baxter graced us with her presence at the party on a cold and rainy day. She added a much needed sparkle to the proceedings. Although it could not be considered a major success, it was better than nothing and made a small contribution to the much-needed funds.

* * * * *

At the end of the year, I was approached by the Starlight Foundation to help with annual fundraising plans. An Englishman named Peter Samuelson had formed the organization in 1982 after he and his cousin, actress Emma Samms, were inspired by a young child battling an inoperable brain tumor. Emma was best known for her role on the daytime soap opera *General Hospital* as well as for replacing Pamela Sue Martin in prime time on *Dynasty*.

Fulfilling the wishes of critically or terminally ill children was the main objective, so here at least was a charity where sympathy ranked high and equally it was hoped, the subsequent donations. Their event outranked others, but mismanagement within the organization created some confusing situations and it couldn't be called an unmitigated success. An embarrassing moment created by the table centerpieces didn't help. Donated by a local florist and looking very pretty with candles in the center, I took a sample to the Beverly Hills Fire Department when to my extreme chagrin it caught fire right there in the office!! Obviously, amendments had to be made to that design.

Equally embarrassing, but in reverse, at a production meeting in 1990 leading up to AFI's David Lean Tribute, the same Beverly Hills Fire Department was late because they had a fire to put out.

* * * * *

Parents Anonymous, with whom we had worked briefly on the documentary *Who Stole My Childhood*, got in touch with me about a fundraiser they were planning for later in the year. It was interesting to note the behavioral differences between one client and another. Most were very accommodating and appreciative, but PA didn't really fit that mold. Maybe it was because this was an organization dedicated to helping dysfunctional families and was thus always surrounded by negativity, but it became one of the most depressing projects for me. Their meetings were held in different locales all over the place, from Disney Studios in Burbank to a location out in a place called Carson, which was close to thirty miles from my office. My work went unappreciated, never mind the mandatory expense reports for gas and so on. I must have been spoiled by other clients, but I learnt the hard way on this one and from then on added "expenses to be reimbursed" in all my contracts.

As time wore on, the meetings became less convenient and, worse, less productive and more and more a waste of time. Cooperation between the personnel at PA and frustrated vendors trying to design the invitation and program book led to an unimaginative outcome with critique high and moral low. This friction also affected the ladies committee, no member of which really wanted to *do* anything. In addition, the location staff at the venue itself proved to be quite unhelpful and uncooperative. On the night of the party, in an effort to save money, the flowers arranged by the volunteers were dead before they reached the tables and the so-called Maitre D' paid no attention to how the room should be set up. Other than that, it was fine.

* * * * *

I felt it somewhat ironic that at the ripe old age of forty-four, I should be asked to work on a fundraiser for the Alzheimer's Foundation. It turned out to be a memorable and somewhat emotional event. Rita Hayworth had died in 1987, and her daughter Yasmin Aga Khan wanted to draw attention to the disease that had taken her life. It was almost a sense of relief to the family when Hayworth was diagnosed with Alzheimer's, as it was deemed more respectable than alcoholism, which had plagued her for many, many years and drawn much bad publicity.

A party celebrating Miss Hayworth's extraordinary life and career was to be held at the St. James Club, an upscale hotel on the Sunset Strip in West Hollywood. Considered to be one of the best examples of Art Deco design in the country, the original opening had taken place in 1931, but as the years went by the building deteriorated and was finally rescued and restored in 1985. Subsequently becoming a most impressive building, it had been placed on the National Register of Historic Places in 1980 and eventually ended up as the Sunset Tower Hotel.

We had a good event there at the end of May, but as with any kind of adult disease (children were a different matter), there was no major outpouring of support or sympathy. The best part for me was working with a man named Arthur Novell, a public relations genius who had represented various underwriters for AFI tributes, and Jim Henson, famous for being the creator of the Muppets. Arthur had an amazing sense of humor and an innate ability to say the right thing at the right time, even though it might be somewhat controversial. He was very much his own man going his own way in a totally uncontrollable world, and it was great to work with him.

* * * * *

To me there was nothing more enjoyable than going to someone else's party. It was such a relief not to worry about what might go awry, who was seated at the wrong table or in the wrong theatre seat, whether the valet parking was working properly, if the wait service wasn't what it should be, and so on. Whatever went wrong, in short, was not my problem. But it was impossible not to judge other people's work and think about how I might have done a task better. It was on such an occasion in October 1988 that I went to the perfect party – as a guest!

The Beverly Hilton Hotel was owned by Merv Griffin then, and this occasion was to celebrate a major renovation just completed to celebrate the brand new look of the Ballroom. The room was filled to capacity with at least 1,200 guests seated at tables of ten. The food and wine were superb. Tom Selleck, riding high as television's Magnum, P.I., was at the next table. There was a terrific show with Mr. Griffin himself giving us a song or two. The only thing I didn't care for was the new carpet. Enormous red roses, combined with other vibrant colors, detracted from the otherwise quite elegant room, but maybe it had been designed to absorb the inevitable spillage of red wine. Anyway, it looked as if it would wear well. Nothing went wrong and I remember it as being one of the most delightful evenings I experienced when not in charge.

Chapter Six 89

* * * * *

On another occasion, at a meeting with the manager of the San Diego Convention Center, I was invited to attend another party given by someone else. It just happened that the day of my appointment coincided with a big event taking place the following evening, and everyone was all excited about it. My meeting related to future parties, so the suggestion I attend the upcoming event was a wonderful introduction to the group. It would also give me the perfect opportunity to observe the difference between a big city project and a more suburban approach. Thinking my events in Los Angeles would be far more sophisticated than a local gathering proved that I couldn't have been more wrong!!

"Tribute to Dance" was just that, and dress rehearsals were taking place as I left with technicians hammering on the set and electrical personnel busy with wiring and complicated lighting. It looked spectacular, and I wondered what to expect from such elaborate preparation.

It turned out to be a fabulous evening and not in the least "countrified." The production could have stood up for itself in any of the most sophisticated of cities. Included in the entertainment were the top singer/dancers from several decades, including Shirley MacLaine, Ann-Margret, Liza Minnelli, Sammy Davis, Jr., Paula Abdul, Ann Miller, the Nicholas Brothers, Juliet Prowse, and Cyd Charisse. I was duly impressed!

* * * * *

At the very end of the 1980's, February 12, 1989, to be exact, the 25th anniversary of director David Lean's classic *Lawrence of Arabia* was celebrated with a restored version of the film screened at the Century City Cineplex theatre in Los Angeles. I had seen it during its first release, of course, and always felt Peter O'Toole was like a beautiful painting. I never forgot the scene in which he paces wildly on the roof of a train, white robes swirling around him and those incredible blue eyes flashing with exhilaration as he is silhouetted against an equally impressive blue sky.

At the reception afterwards, I bumped into Anthony Andrews who remembered the Jack Lemmon Tribute the previous year and thanked me once again for getting him a ticket at the last minute. Also sprinkling their star qualities were Michael York of *Cabaret* fame, Alan Alda (Captain Hawkeye in *M*A*S*H*), and Michael Douglas then perhaps best known for his production credits on *One Flew Over the Cuckoo's Nest* as well as having famous father, Kirk.

In the same year AFI crowned David Lean with the Life Achievement Award. That was another highly memorable event, and the film clips were absolutely mesmerizing – *Lawrence of Arabia*, quite possibly his best known film had been preceded by *The Bridge on the River Kwai* and even before that probably my favorite film of all time, *Brief Encounter*, which was actually older than I was. The Dickens classics *Great Expectations* and *Oliver Twist* led to *Dr. Zhivago* and *Ryan's Daughter*, and the list went on and on. It was a classic example of a director being responsible for a far more varied and interesting career than most actors though if asked, the majority of the population today would not know his name.

Sir David was admired by the entire industry. Producers, fellow directors, cinematographers, crewmembers, actors or extras – all looked up to him as one of the greatest. And it showed in the turnout for him. From young to maturing (I refrain from using the word "old"), they were all there to pay their respects.

Chapter Six

Fellow directors Steven Spielberg, Arthur Hiller (probably best remembered for *Love Story*, Ryan O'Neal and Ali MacGraw's tragic tale from 1970), and the 1986 Life Achievement Award recipient Billy Wilder of *Some Like It Hot* fame, were all there to cheer him on

Kirstie Alley, Goldie Hawn, Milton Berle, Sid Caesar, Rich Little, Steve Martin, and Telly Sevalas, so memorable as *Kojak* in the 1970s, were all there. Representing drama and comedy were Pam Dawber from *Mork and Mindy* and her husband Mark Harmon whose portrayal of Special Agent Leroy Gibbs in *NCIS* would become legendary.

Among the stars applauding, Angelica Huston represented her famous family and former recipients of the award, Gene Kelly and Jack Lemmon, with his friend and neighbor Walter Matthau were also among the admirers. Anthony Newley flew in from London.

The prolific composer of movie themes from many major motion pictures including *Lawrence of Arabia*, Maurice Jarre paid homage, and one of the most famous cinematographers of all time, Vilmos Zsigmond graced the evening with his presence. He was perhaps best remembered for *Close Encounters of the Third Kind*, for which he had won an Oscar in 1977.

Producers Albert "Cubby" Broccoli, famous for the James Bond movies, joined Stephen Cannel, the prolific writer of TV hits like *Ironside*, *Columbo*, and *The Rockford Files* to add to the applause, as did publicist Ronni Chasen, who attended every year, always telling me how important it was that she be seated well. Little did we know that ten years later she would be shot to death on Sunset Boulevard as she made her way home from a movie premiere, in what was later determined to be a random act of violence.

Finally, the after-party glowed with Stefanie Powers of *Hart to Hart* fame; Shelley Winters, who had been so courageous in *The Poseidon Adventure*; Rich Little, the comic impersonator nicknamed "The Man of a Thousand Voices;" and James Fox who had been named Most Promising Newcomer for his role in one of Harold Pinter's early masterpieces *The Servant* starring English actor of the famous *Dr.* comedies Dirk Bogarde. It was truly a star-studded evening.

* * * * *

At the end of 1987, I was living sky-high in the hills above Los Angeles close to the world-famous HOLLYWOOD sign, just minutes away from Griffith Park. This was a new location for me, so it seemed natural that I would be approached to help with a new award show. This time comedy was king, and producer/director/writer George Schlatter was in charge. First known for creating the breakthrough comedy series *Laugh In*, George had by then established an extraordinary reputation in a number of fields and won innumerable awards. Not resting on his laurels, he created the American Comedy Awards. This was to be a group of awards presented annually in the United States recognizing performances and performers in the comedy field, from both television and film. Having been involved with award shows for some time, I was a natural choice to be asked to help out. George himself had a wonderful sense of humor, and the production meetings were very funny although I committed what I found out later to be a cardinal sin during one them, when I interrupted him with what I thought was a necessary comment. He didn't appreciate it one bit, and I was never asked to work with him again. The show was a success and was held annually for many years, but regretfully without me.

* * * * *

New clients started popping up at this time, one of whom was the Joffrey Ballet Company from Chicago. This would prove to be a wonderful association, especially as on their initial engagement they were accompanied by the Bolshoi Ballet, making a rare visit from Russia. Because of possible defections, which had happened in the past, the troupe was closely watched at all times by KGB officers. It was a fearsome sight to see these big burly Russian security men with guns backstage at the Music Center, waiting to pounce on some disenchanted ballerina who didn't want to go home. That was the first time I had to go through a metal detector to get through the stage door.

There was a special VIP reception before the Bolshoi's performance on the evening of August 14, 1987. Their presentation was greeted with what I considered to be an overly enthusiastic audience who treated it more like a football game, cheering and clapping at every jump or pirouette. I couldn't help wondering if European audiences behaved the same way, but having no comparison, I had no way of knowing. It seemed to me there was more applause than dance.

On opening night for the Joffrey, their performance was followed by a Gala Dinner on the mezzanine level of the Ahmanson Theatre, one of the three auditoriums comprising the Music Center in downtown Los Angeles. The other two theatres were the Dorothy Chandler Pavilion and the Mark Taper Forum. Everyone looked elegant in black tie. The setting was wonderful, but the catering and service left a lot to be desired. It was somewhat nerve-wracking to watch the waiters still setting up tables and putting out the salt and pepper shakers during the last intermission before the final curtain. But overall it was a big success, and I was out until 1:30 am. At least there was no traffic on the Hollywood freeway at that time. Ironically, for once not having to set the alarm, I was woken up just after 7 o'clock the following morning by a relatively strong earthquake so there was certainly no rest for the wicked.

The Joffrey Ballet's next appearance in October was met with the same enthusiasm as the first, but the catering service was worse than before. It was so frustrating after working so hard and having innumerable meetings and tastings and approving sample floral decorations, when nothing was the same on the night of! The food was dreadful, on some tables the flower arrangements actually toppled over, the lighting was all wrong, and the service again proved interminably slow. However, it was probably only my staff and I who noticed. The guests had a lovely time, and at least the champagne was chilled!

The following year, on December 23, 1988, the Joffrey returned to Los Angeles for its premier performance of *The Nutcracker*, followed by a patron dinner for five hundred guests. This would become an annual tradition, and it became increasingly challenging to find truly festive centerpieces for each table. That first year we outdid ourselves with an absolutely beautiful wooden rocking horse about 24 inches tall, decorated with ornaments, miniatures, tinsel, tiny lights, little wrapped packages, and ribbons. At the end of the evening, they were auctioned off and sent home to the lucky bidders. This added greatly to the fundraising results, but it also meant that my assistant and I had to spend several hours packaging up the goods in big boxes to be picked up the next day for delivery. They were too big and fragile to be hand carried. I got home at 2:15am when again, there was virtually no traffic on the Hollywood Freeway. I timed myself and it took precisely eight minutes from door to door, when on an average day it would take twenty minutes, and with traffic even longer.

Chapter Seven:
In The Studio,
Out Of Town, And On The Road!

It was during my tenure at Liberty Records that one of the most exciting musical events of my life occurred.

It was my birthday, April 11, 1966, and Dave Pell, one of the A&R (Artists and Repertoire) guys, asked me if I would like to go to a live recording session that evening. Of course I said yes and thought how exciting is that! Dave knew that I shared an apartment with two other English girls and said I could bring them along if they were interested. All young and eager to experience just about anything, we were very excited by the prospect and went off to the address of the studio. When we arrived, a large sign reading "CLOSED SESSION" greeted us, but apparently it wasn't closed to us, so in we went. A large open room had a single microphone at one end, a large control panel for the recording engineers at the other end, and in the middle four empty high back chairs. The three of us sat down and waited.

In walked Frank Sinatra!

We were flabbergasted and, as the Brits would say, "gob-smacked." He paid no attention to us or anyone else other than the technical people. He was totally focused and even Mia Farrow, his wife at the time, and for whom the fourth chair had been provided, couldn't divert his attention. Not that she tried, but she never did sit down and flitted about in the background never actually landing anywhere.

Nelson Riddle's arrangement had been pre-recorded, eliminating the need for the studio to be full of musicians and after a bit of banter with the engineers, Mr. Sinatra did the first take. Little did I know at the time what he chose to record on that memorable occasion would become a classic. The song he sang was "Strangers In The Night." To this day, when I hear it I get goose bumps, remembering that I was there in the studio with only a handful of other people as the Chairman of the Board recorded one of his most famous numbers. The flip side (they had 45's in those days) was an upbeat version of "The Most Beautiful Girl in the World," which wasn't my favorite, but it was Frank Sinatra and none of us minded in the least. He could have sung the phone book for all we cared! What a way to celebrate a birthday!

An earlier Frank Sinatra experience took place shortly after I arrived in the US over the weekend of December 4-6, 1964, when early on the Friday morning, my fellow Brit roommates and a friend from Denver drove our newly acquired 1957 Chevrolet convertible from Hollywood to Las Vegas. We were headed for the Sands Hotel, where Mr. Sinatra was appearing. In those days you didn't stand much chance of getting into any show room if you weren't staying at the same hotel, and even that could be tricky when someone of major status was appearing.

The Copa Room at the Sands was famous for its entertainers, especially the Rat Pack. Frank Sinatra, Dean Martin, Sammy Davis, Jr., Peter Lawford, Joey Bishop, and sometimes Shirley MacLaine would turn up and add impromptu repartee when any one of them was appearing. Sometimes you got all of them!

We couldn't afford to stay at the Sands the entire weekend, so had reserved for Sunday only and with limited funds, were pulling a familiar trick at another hotel for Friday and Saturday nights. We booked one double room with twin beds and put the mattresses on the floor, thus allowing four to sleep in relative comfort on either the box spring or the mattress! Split up this way, the room charge became much more affordable. Two of us checked in and once we knew the room number, the other two would come up the back stairs, as it were.

On this occasion after successfully checking into the Stardust Hotel on the Strip for the massive sum of $10 per night (split four ways), we began our weekend experience.

I must say it was like chalk and cheese moving from the Stardust to the Sands, which we accomplished with no problem on Sunday morning. We then phoned the reservation office from our room to confirm we were down for the midnight show and asked if we could make a request. Claiming we had come all the way from England to see Mr. Sinatra, and in our best British accents, asked if he would please sing "A Nightingale Sang In Berkeley Square."

During the afternoon the phone rang in our room and a voice said this was the Sinatra office and they were confirming our attendance and the song requested for later that night. Of course this threw us into a blind panic as to why such a call should have been made. What did it mean, would he really sing our request, would we get preferred seating, and why would they call if not to do something special? Our conjecture lasted the rest of the day.

Finally, it came time to go to the show. We had checked out of the hotel and everything was stashed in the car as we all had to be at work Monday morning, so were planning to drive back to Los Angeles right after the midnight show, which we calculated would be at approximately 2am – what you do in your youth!!!!

The Maître D' consulted a list when we got to the top of the line and muttered something to the Captain, who was to lead us to the table.

I should add here that virtually all show rooms in Las Vegas at that time had table seating, as opposed to theatre style. Rectangular tables for six to eight people faced the stage at the front of the room, behind which and raised up a step or two would be a ring of highly upholstered booths for four or six guests. Following the same format, on the next tier up rectangular tables were placed on the rail with booths behind and so it went on for various levels.

Coming in from the rear of the house and heading for the stage, we dreaded being shown a booth at the very back so were pleased to be led down to the next level. Then we went further to the next level which was much better, but didn't stop there and we couldn't believe how close we were getting to the stage. To our incredulous delight we were shown to one of two tables right *on* the stage!! They were facing each other on either side and standing solo in the center barely ten feet away was the microphone at which the great man himself would be standing.

Barely controlling our intense excitement, we ordered 2 bottles of champagne (the minimum requirement for the midnight show) and prepared for the great moment.

Beginning with Count Basie, everything was incredible. It couldn't have been better, and Frank did sing "A Nightingale Sang In Berkeley Square." We all thought he looked over at our table several times, which must have been wishful thinking, but since we all thought it, maybe it was true. Anyway, we chose to believe it.

But it got even better! At the very end of the evening, a waiter came over to our table and whispered "Compliments of the Sands Hotel, ladies"!

Chapter Seven

Talk about surprises – did life get any better?! Did that mean I could say Frank Sinatra bought me a drink one night?! We didn't drive back to Los Angeles - we flew on Cloud 9!

I always felt you could tell how Frank Sinatra's personal life was going by the way he sang. When things were going well, he had a wonderful *joie de vivre* about his performance, joking and laughing, smoking and drinking. If all was not great with his world, it seemed to me he performed a bit like a zombie, going through the motions and frequently singing off key. I saw him like that a couple of times and of course could be completely wrong on this. It was just how I felt and maybe how I would have performed under similar circumstances, and maybe that's how everyone behaves, be it in show business, sports, or the corporate world.

I did meet Frank Sinatra personally a few times and shook his hand once, but it was always a case of "the lights are on but nobody's home" as he was clearly bored by being introduced to what he would have called "nobodies" because they wanted to say they had met him. However, he provided two of the greatest memories of my life – it's too bad I never had the chance to say thank you.

* * * * *

One sunny August morning in 1970, I once again made my way to Las Vegas, Nevada. My English friend Sue was working for a public relations firm at the time, and one of her clients was a young actress named Janet MacLachlan. Janet was making a guest appearance in the TV series *The Name of the Game,* and we were going to watch her scenes being filmed at the International Hotel (now the Hilton). The series starred Tony Franciosa, Gene Barry, and Robert Stack. Janet had a scene with Tony to be shot in the morning. We were introduced to Mr.

Franciosa afterwards and felt duly impressed by his charm and good looks!

For lunch we gathered in the VIP dining room, and I found myself sitting next to Sammy Davis, Jr.! He was in wonderful form, very funny, and kept the entire table enraptured with his stories and jokes despite frequent interruptions from fans requesting his autograph. He never got impatient or seemed to resent being disturbed, and eventually I asked him if he really didn't mind this constant invasion of his privacy? He said the day he got annoyed by such intrusions would be the day he got out of show business. He added that he needed the fans as much as they needed him and was never going to forget that. Neither were any of us going to forget our very own Sammy Davis, Jr. show.

The first time I saw Sammy Davis, Jr. was at the London Palladium on April 22, 1963. I thought he was fabulous. Little did I think then that I would ever meet him, let alone have a personal conversation!

Mr. Davis spent his entire life in show business. He was multi-talented to say the least. He could sing, dance, and act in the theatre and on film and do amazing impersonations. I never heard anyone sing "Mr. Bojangles" like he did.

He was also part of the famous Rat Pack, along with Frank Sinatra, Dean Martin, Joey Bishop, and Peter Lawford, and although I saw him several times performing alone, even at one of his opening nights at the Sands in 1971, regrettably I didn't have the privilege of being present when others in the group joined in, which according to all reports, were hilarious occasions.

Sammy Davis, Jr. was one of the recipients of the Kennedy Center Honors in 1987 and won accolades his entire life, well and truly deserving his nickname "Mister Show Business."

That August day in Las Vegas led from one incredible experience to another as the afternoon scenes of *The Name of the Game* had the cast performing in a number with Ike and Tina Turner.

Janet MacLachlan created quite a scandal around that time by becoming a single mother and producing a daughter she named Samantha. She never revealed the name of the father and of course rumors ran rampant, one being he was a prominent political figure. She never did reveal his name, so I guess we'll never know.

The evening became even more fantastic when we went on to see Elvis Presley's show and had a table right at the front of the showroom up against the stage. Elvis was in his prime in 1970. In his white skintight leather outfit with a glittering collar framing his sweating brow, we were completely blown away. To this day I have never experienced such an incredibly sexy and exciting show.

* * * * *

In the summer of 1977, I flew to England for a holiday It was a great time to visit as it marked Queen Elizabeth's Silver Jubilee and lots of parties and processions were taking place all over the country to celebrate the 25th anniversary of her reign. The actual Jubilee Day was Tuesday, June 7, to coincide with her official birthday. I went into the heart of London to watch the Royal Golden Coach pass by with the Queen giving her regal wave. I remember she was wearing a pink hat.

That trip was memorable in more ways than one. A friend who worked in law and represented some very interesting clients, mostly dealing with divorces, had one in particular who was a real character. Lord Spencer "Spenny" Compton (pronounced Cumpton) was heir to a British peerage and shortly thereafter became the 7th Marquess of

Northampton, with an ancestral home worthy of the most aristocratic of families, namely Castle Ashby.

Situated in the East Midlands in the county of Northamptonshire, the main house is surrounded by two hundred acres of parkland designed by Capability Brown, known as "England's greatest gardener" after he designed more than 150 parks in the eighteenth century. Given to the Compton family in 1512 by Henry VIII, the driveway alone is over a mile long and the entire estate covers more than 10,000 acres. Open to the public during the summer months, Elizabeth (my friend, not the Queen) and I were to be given a private tour when we were invited for the day on Monday, June 6. Spenny had arranged to meet us at The Falcon, the local village pub, and if we got there first to order him his "usual." He made a spectacular entrance as we had indeed beaten him to it, and it was very quaint and utterly charming to hear all the locals addressing him as "M'Lord" when they spoke. It turned out the family owned the entire village as well as the pub and his "usual" was a pint of best bitter.

We went back to the house and met Rosie, soon to be Spenny's third wife (of six so far), and their yellow Labrador and new puppies born just three days earlier. A tour of the house made us feel very privileged and important as we went into the areas where the family lived and the general public was not allowed. One of the highlights of the day came when Spenny pulled out some of the family jewels and we tried on rings, which had previously been owned and worn by Mary Queen of Scots! I felt as though I had walked into the history books.

Later that week we met him again for a visit to Annabel's in Berkeley Square, the famous London members-only nightclub whose patrons included Prince Charles, Princess Anne, and according to the local newspapers, quite often Princess Diana and Sarah Fergusson. American visitors included Richard Nixon, Aristotle Onassis, and Frank Sinatra. It was quite something to enter those hallowed halls, and only because Spenny was a member were we permitted to go in. Our entrance wasn't terribly dignified, however, as by then we had all been imbibing gallons of champagne and while waiting Spenny kept sliding down the wall! Refreshed once inside, we had a fabulous time and I felt very "in with the in crowd!"

* * * * *

On Monday, September 30, 1985, I flew to Charlottesville, Virginia to coordinate the logistics of a weekend house party at the palatial estate of John and Patricia Kluge. It turned out to be one of the best and most memorable events I ever experienced.

Clive David, with whom I had worked on the "Los Angeles Men and Women of Achievement" project in earlier years, was in charge once again, and it was a pleasure to help out in my small way on all the details of what would be a very complicated weekend of festivities.

John and Patricia Kluge were considered royalty in Virginia. They were sky high in the financial world, and in 1981 Forbes listed John at #4 in the list of the Top 5 Wealthiest Americans.

John and Patricia had been married in 1981. After several years renovating Albemarle House, an existing Georgian mansion, and adding two enormous wings, they wanted to celebrate by giving a housewarming party. Covering enormous acreage, the estate sat just outside Charlottesville. To reach it you first had to drive past Monticello, the renowned plantation home of Thomas Jefferson, the third president of the United States.

To match the glamor and grandeur of the estate, this was to be an unparalleled and exotic party given on the grandest scale. Afterwards, in Betty Beale's Society Column in *The Washington Post*, the headline ran "At Kluges' estate, a memorable gala." The *Richmond Times-Dispatcher* declared, "In Albemarle, the traditions are rich and the rich are traditions."

There was to be a black-tie dinner party on the evening of Friday, October 25, followed the next day by a picnic lunch on the lawns in front of the house, a barbecue and cabaret in one of the barns on Saturday evening complete with farm animals lining the walkway into cocktails, and finally Sunday brunch overlooking one of the lakes complete with bagpipes to serenade the departure and conclusion of their extraordinary weekend. There were two lakes I should add, one with white and one with black "swans a swimming."

The journey from Los Angeles several weeks before the event called for a change of planes in Washington, where we got on a little fourteen-seat prop plane which was so small you could hardly stand up. However, it delivered us safely in just 25 minutes to Charlottesville airport, where one of the Kluge chauffeurs was waiting on the tarmac with a gleaming Mercedes to drive us to what would be our new home until the party weekend was over. We would share with the chef a lodge on the grounds a mile or so from the main house, with five bedrooms and five baths. Each morning we would leave a shopping list at the foot of the stairs for groceries required for our evening's dinner. It was marvelous to dream up exotic dishes without having to worry about the price tag or stand in line at the check out counter.

On our first evening, we barely had time to dump our suitcases in respective bedrooms before being collected to go to the main house to dine with the Kluges. I will never forget that first dinner. Getting to Albemarle House was spectacular in itself, as once through the electric gates, the drive of over a mile wound through the recently opened golf course and past various lakes, all the while surrounded by forests of trees and lush vegetation.

The butler, a rather fierce little Englishman named Raybould, "greeted" us at the front door, with a look of great disdain before we were shown into the drawing room where we were met by John Kluge. We were told later that Raybould had recently graduated from Butler School and was playing the role to the hilt! Mr. Kluge, by complete contrast, was warm and friendly and offered us a drink, which Raybould duly presented on a silver tray. I requested a glass of white wine, which I thought was a safe bet, but later was to discover the lady of the house drank champagne almost exclusively, so I soon switched to that, which was my preference anyway

For dinner, there were just the four of us in the enormous formal dining room, which seated at least thirty guests at a long table stretching the entire length of one of the new wings, which created the "U" shaped design of the house. I remember having a mental picture of a lone couple seated for dinner at either end and sending the saltshaker careening all the way down the middle of the table. Our first course was a hot soup served in a small bowl with a cover. I couldn't think what I was supposed to do with this very thoughtful but rather inconvenient cover, as the mahogany table had no mats, was polished to a mirror gleam and the contents of the bowl positively steaming. I watched Patricia, who just abandoned hers, sort of tilted on to a side plate, so I followed suit. Mrs. Kluge had a button beneath her right foot to summon the servers when needed, and I remember feeling very intimidated and uncomfortable to begin with. But John was very charming, and Patricia extremely enthusiastic about the upcoming party, so that soon wore off.

Clive and I were each given a Mercedes to drive and office space on the estate at "the Farm" to work in. Looking at the beautiful surroundings of rolling hills, forests of trees, countless rhododendron bushes, all in the peace and quiet of the country, it was hard to believe I was paid to be there. Having established residency in the new office and installing Clive's word processor in a place of prominence, we set to work figuring out what to do first from the myriad of tasks awaiting action. That opening day was taken up with moving into this lovely office overlooking one of the lakes and was made even more memorable by an introduction to Achilles, the ten-week-old puppy who was the latest addition to the family.

The next day was spent at the local hotel in Charlottesville, where all seventy guest rooms had been reserved by the Kluges for the party weekend. Although Albemarle House was large, there was not a huge number of bedrooms, and only a few couples could be accommodated there, so the remaining guests were to reside at the Boars Head Inn. Travel arrangements included the charter of two DC-9 jets to pick up and deliver people from New York to Charlottesville, as well as any number of cars and busses to take them to and from the Boars Head Inn. In addition, there were 27 private planes flying in from all over the world, as well as a few passengers on commercial aircraft. This made arrival and departure schedules somewhat complicated.

On our second evening we were invited to Albemarle House again for dinner, but this time it was far less formal and Patricia, Clive, and I ate in the kitchen in front of a roaring fire. Later on, we moved into the media room, where one huge screen was surrounded by three smaller monitors so you could watch no fewer than four television shows at the same time. On the big screen we watched *Dynasty,* starring John Forsythe and Linda Evans, the popular prime time soap opera revolving around the Carringtons of Denver, an incredibly wealthy family, which seemed ironic as I felt we were living it for real in Virginia with the Kluges.

Another outing took us by private jet to Washington for an all-day meeting with the famous catering firm of Ridgewells, which was to provide all the food and beverages, rentals, decorations, and so on for the entire weekend. Driven by one of the chauffeurs to the private part of Charlottesville airport and literally right to the steps leading up into the plane, it was the first time I had experienced that type of flying. "Don't get used to it," I thought as we took off without tickets or queues to deal with, in incredible comfort and the whole plane to ourselves.

At Ridgewells, we tasted various combinations of lunches and dinners. Patricia was very particular as to what she wanted, if not always as practical. At one point she had suggested swan for a dinner entrée, but this had been vetoed by pretty much everyone as being just a touch too controversial, not to mention fairly tasteless. I had never had swan so couldn't contribute much, though I did say I didn't think it would look too good on a printed menu. We also had to approve flower arrangements, interior tent decorations, and color schemes. This was a massive undertaking, and when the weekend finally arrived I took a photograph of the convoy of eleven Ridgewell trucks coming up the driveway the morning of Friday, October 25 as they proceeded to Albemarle House with their fabulous fare.

At the end of the day, we stopped in New York at JFK Airport to pick up John – another interesting experience. I remember watching his car weave its way through lots of other private planes before depositing him at the steps of his. I was also impressed by a cordless phone in the cabin from which you could call anywhere in the world – an impressive feat in 1985! I didn't want to think about my return flight on a commercial plane after this was all over, as I would be in economy on American Airlines. We were all somewhat exhausted from a very busy day and, anticipating our weariness, were given dinner in the main house, but on our own this time, although still waited on by a butler.

There were so many details to work on that I started a "To Do Book" but gave up after I got to #61.

One particular evening proved traumatic to say the least. The central heating had yet to be repaired in our guest house, and the weather had turned chilly so we decided to put a couple of logs in the fireplace. As the house had not been lived in for a while, things were inclined to stick and such was the case with the flue up the chimney, which was stuck in the closed position. After unknowingly lighting it, we were forced to throw water on the flames. This created thick smoke and then we discovered the windows had been painted shut and it was only thanks to the front door opening wide and our finding a fan we got the situation under control.

On Sunday, October 6, it was Patricia's 38th birthday. We were invited to celebrate the occasion at the house just the four of us. Vintage pink champagne and wild boar were on the menu – another first for me. Afterwards, we all adjourned to the new disco in the basement. Complete with a mirrored ball in the center of the ceiling throwing diamonds of light all over the room and a DJ machine providing the right music, we were obliged to dance! I must say I felt a bit idiotic jigging about on a huge dance floor with just three other people, two of whom (John and Clive) were not enthusiastic at all, but Patricia was having a lovely time.

The disco, reputed to have cost a million dollars, converted to a screening room, which I found much more to my taste. Patricia's love for champagne was revealed by her design of the extremely comfortable chairs, whose arms cradled the base of a champagne glass to perfection!

To emphasize the "other world" in which we were living, one day Clive, John and Sharonette, the nanny, with Les, another butler, all flew to New York in the private plane, to have fittings for new uniforms to be worn over the big weekend. Other signs of the incredible affluence within this household, which we were told employed no fewer than 198 staff members, included a model of the Statue of Liberty. Almost hidden under the curve of the stairs this was not a model of the one finally chosen because, according to the family story, that was deemed too sexy although it still evoked a unique historic significance. Then there were the chandeliers in the stables, which one of the grooms told us were much more beautiful than those at Windsor Castle. I never was quite sure if he meant the chandeliers in the stables or in the Castle! There was a helicopter pad, and ground was to be broken shortly on a chapel. The grass seed was just emerging on the golf course, not to mention a framed check for a *billion* dollars hanging on a wall in the living room where Clive and I were staying.

On another occasion I spent a considerable amount of time at the Boars Head Inn evaluating the accommodations. It would be my job to allocate the guest rooms in an appropriate fashion. However, since everyone would expect nothing but the best to match their egos, it was not an easy task. This proved only too true as we got closer to the date, when I had a call from a particularly highly regarded (by himself) executive who had his assistant check with me to make sure he would be staying in the Presidential Suite. The Boars Head Inn didn't have a Presidential Suite, but I assured his office that he would. After hanging up, I immediately placed a call to the hotel requesting they make "Presidential Suite" plaques and ensure that one was placed on each and every guest room door.

On Monday, October 14, less than two weeks before the party, the scandal broke! It seemed the *Daily Mail* in England had unearthed a story detailing how Patricia had worked in her early career as a nude model for first husband Russell Gay at *Knave* magazine. There were revealing shots of her belly dancing as well as descriptive explanations detailing a "personal" column she had written at the time, answering letters about the seamier side of sex lives, as well as full frontal nude pictures, which had supposedly appeared in the *Knave* publication. To make matters worse, Patricia was to attend a Palm Beach charity gala the following month where she was to be seated next to Prince Charles. Needless to say, that was not to be and the Kluges did not attend, but they went ahead with their own party, though with somewhat dampened spirits.

An embarrassing *faux pas* I made, although not in the same league as Patricia's, happened one day as Clive was leaving the office. His parting shot as he hurried out was a request that I phone the Queen of one of the European countries who was on the guest list and check if she was bringing her son. The number was in his book, he said, as he disappeared through the door. I duly dialed the number without any further thought than to inquire about the son as requested but when the Palace phone was answered my mind went a complete blank and all I could think of to say was *'hello, I'm calling from the United States – is the Queen there?"* Fortunately, the person at the other end did not take offense, instead I heard a muffled laugh and then was told, Her Majesty was in fact out and could he take a message. I was mortified at my lack of decorum and extremely relieved that no one else was in the office to hear, duly left the message and hung up the phone.

As we got closer to the date, more personnel were flown in to cope with the extra work. Clive had a group of helpers for times like these, and I must say it was a wonderful perk for me. With a week to go, a calligrapher joined us, as place cards were required for most of the gatherings. The money spent on this party was mindboggling, and I wasn't really sure any reasoning could justify it. But I was having such a good time and so thoroughly enjoying it all that I decided not to try.

Finally, the weekend arrived and guests began to assemble flying in on the chartered jets, their own private planes, and even commercial airliners. The only couple that didn't make it were Mr. and Mrs. Norman Mailer, who had an accident en route to La Guardia Airport in New York.

Friday's black-tie dinner was held in an elaborate tent constructed in the courtyard between the two new wings of the house. The calligrapher had done her stuff with the place cards. The decorations were spectacular and the food extraordinary. On this occasion we (the staff) were not permitted to sit with the guests and were dispatched to the kitchen. However, as it turned out we had the best of it since earlier in the day Clive and Patricia had a major altercation about the protective plastic walls of the tent. At her insistence and to his chagrin, they were taken away as she didn't like the way they looked. This meant everyone was very cold but nobody was brave enough to admit it. We, however, were cozy by the fire in the kitchen.

It was reputed to have cost $150,000 just for this one tent, but it showed, even with the sides removed. There were some ninety guests, including royals, celebrities, and senior executives, as well as prominent citizens from all over the world. Sir David Frost was among the guests. I remembered him well from my teenage years, when he hosted the satirical and extraordinarily clever BBC television series *That Was the Week That Was.* Everything came to a halt at the allotted hour so that all could watch. Later in his extraordinarily successful and varied career, he would become best known for his intuitive interviews with prominent figures like Richard Nixon after his resignation. Impresario Lord Lew Grade, another Brit who was responsible for the newly created ITV network, had also flown in to join the illustrious group.

Entertainers Tony Bennett, whose most famous hit had to be "I Left My Heart In San Francisco," and Vic Damone, who according to the latest gossip was dating Diahann Carroll (of television's *Julia* fame) at the time were both in attendance. Word had it that Mr. Damone's long distance phone bills could match some of the other more exotic expenses and then some. Opera singer Beverly Sills made a glamorous addition to the group, looking every bit the star she had become as she chatted with Richard Zanuck and his production company partner David Brown. The Zanuck/Brown team had a number of well-known films to their credit including *The Sting* (1973), starring Paul Newman and Robert Redford, and *Jaws* (1975) with Richard Dreyfuss and Roy Scheider. They would later go on to produce the Academy Award-winning *Driving Miss Daisy* in 1990, starring Jessica Tandy and Morgan Freeman. David's wife Helen Gurley Brown was the editor-in-chief of *Cosmopolitan* magazine and wrote "Sex and the Single Girl," which well and truly shocked the 1960s! Ann Getty came without her famous husband Gordon who had inherited his father (oil tycoon J. Paul's) billion-dollar trust and could be seen chatting with Norman and Frances Lear. Mr. Lear was a writer and producer with sitcoms *All in the Family*, *The Jeffersons*, and *Maude* under his belt. Also present were Lord and Lady Ramsey, who added to the British presence. I couldn't help thinking that they possibly felt the most at home as their family residence, Broadlands, was on par with Albemarle House in magnificence.

Saturday brought beautiful weather. The picnic lunch on the expansive lawns in front of Albemarle House was a great success. We were very lucky over the entire weekend, though, for many days prior it had rained and rained and rained, necessitating Plans B, C, D and E!! In the end we didn't need any of them – everyone had a basket full of goodies and wine. During lunch, restored antique carriages were paraded along the drive to the delight of the guests. The harness on the horses competing with the brass wear on the carriages, all gleaming and sparkling in the sun with the drivers appropriately dressed in livery from the past century, made a spectacular addition to the festivities.

For me, Saturday evening was the most fun. Held in a huge barn set between the two lakes, various farm animals had been collected and put in pens along a walkway leading to the main dining area. There were over two hundred guests by this time, and everyone loved it. Elizabeth Taylor and John Warner were enchanted by a young calf housed with its mother, as were newly engaged couple Barbara Walters and Merv Adelson. Other guests could be seen petting the goats, sheep, and horses as they made their way towards cocktails. There was even a mechanical bull, which David Frost was persuaded to ride, and he in fact did quite well. I sat with Ambassador Helene von Damm, former US Ambassador to Austria and her husband while listening to country music singer Mel

Tillis, who provided the entertainment, which was highly appropriate in such a setting.

This same tent by the side of the lake was completely transformed overnight for Sunday's brunch, complete with a different color scheme and decorations plus a new musical group playing medieval tunes. We had changed the clocks overnight (but I had forgotten) and it was a real relief to have an extra hour to get ready for this final act.

As lunch wound down and it became time to think about departure, the finale began. As the guests left the tent ready to go home, there came the faint and haunting sound of Scottish bagpipes from over the brow of a distant hill. The music grew louder but nobody could be seen until at last the pipers became visible cresting the summit and marching down the hill their kilts swinging in the wind. Emotions grew high as the sound increased and the pipers continued on their way with guests applauding in appreciation. It was a spectacularly fitting conclusion to an extraordinary weekend that brought tears to most eyes as the busses made ready to leave.

Clive and I left a couple of days later, but not before Patricia had taken me to one side and offered me a job. In addition, she said they would build me a house on the estate. I regretfully declined having been independent for so many years, although it was a very flattering offer.

At the airport our departure matched the rest of the project as a man in a tuxedo playing the violin serenaded us onto the plane. I was handed a red rose. Too bad American Airlines broke the bottle of wine in my hand luggage. My suitcase suffered several rips. The flight was crowded and the seats uncomfortable, but that had nothing to do with the

Kluges, nor could it tarnish in any way those incredibly memorable weeks in Virginia.

Chapter Eight:
Behind The Scenes

The movie/entertainment business has more people behind the scenes than in front of the camera. That includes me, as well as studio executives, technical people, clerical personnel, production staff, and possibly the most overlooked but equally and perhaps the most important – the writers.

When I first began to use my organizational skills in the 1970s, the most sophisticated equipment I possessed was a word processor. We've come a long way since then, and when I look back at the methods used, although the end result was very often the same, the road to the finish line was strewn with tasks taking hours and hours, which can be accomplished today in minutes and in some cases even seconds.

A major event usually required a lead-time of anywhere from three to four months, beginning with the acquisition of various permits from the city and fire department. Invitations had to be designed and printed, mailing lists put together, the budget organized, press and publicity coverage worked out, location and dates all confirmed (making sure there was no conflict with another major happening), and so on.

In the case of the American Film Institute's Life Achievement Award Tributes, it was up to my office to send the initial invitations, take the responses, and keep a record of the payments for tickets. A special program book would be designed with pages dedicated to the respective honoree and sold for $1,000 each. The production of the television show emanating from the evening would be the responsibility of executive producer George Stevens, Jr., and he and I worked together closely to make sure the celebrities appearing in the show were seated in the appropriate places for camera angles and spontaneous reactions.

As anyone who has ever worked on a special event will tell you, the seating can be a nightmare. Put together the egos in Hollywood, add the order of importance each studio feels it deserves, throw in personal relationships – studio heads and stars alike seemed to change partners every five minutes, – and it can become very tricky!

I would begin the process by creating a large diagram of the Beverly Hilton ballroom or wherever the action would take place. Circles indicated the position and number of tables involved, which for AFI totaled 120. Each one would be assigned a number for easy reference. In the ballroom at the Hilton, there were four levels, beginning with what we called "the floor," which was a square area below the stage. On the next level in a horseshoe shape, two tables one in front of the other would surround "the floor" some four steps up. Behind them another horseshoe of similarly placed tables would wind around the ballroom giving way to the top level, thus allowing great sightlines to the stage from just about everywhere. This particular setup was vastly superior to the other hotels offering similar event space, which mostly consisted of just two levels with those on the second level at the back hardly able to see anything.

With no computer programs available in those days, I devised a system using map flags to denote the location of guests. A pushpin rectangular flag with each name printed on it would be inserted into a foam core board measuring 36" x 30" resting on an easel. Each flag would be placed into the appropriately numbered table.

An additional asset was my color scheme. First there were yellow flags for celebrities. This allowed the producer and director of the television show to ensure that their stars were in camera range. If they weren't, it was a simple matter of moving the flag from one table to another. Next came pale blue flags indicating that a company had purchased an entire table for ten guests, meaning one or two individuals couldn't be moved because the entire table had to stay together. Special VIPs associated with the organization, board members, and so on would have pink flags. Red flags covered the press people, with white ones indicating individual ticket buyers. With over a thousand people attending, this proved to be a simple method of taking in at a glance where everyone was seated.

The entire board would eventually become covered with colored flags, which made for a very good overview of the entire room for all the entities involved. This system sounds old fashioned now that there are sophisticated computer programs available, but it worked very well at the time and made it easy to move guests around as necessary. The end result became a seating book listing all the guests with their allotted table number. To transfer the information from the flags on the board to the book was an incredibly time-consuming operation. The process began by transferring the names of the guests at each table to an individual page in a three-ring binder in chronological order. Then the information for each table number was transferred by hand to a 3" x 5" card and placed in a separate file. The end result was a set of paper-clipped cards listing the name of the guests at each table. For example, at table 301 the top card would say Universal Studios, Table 1 of 2. Behind that, on a separate card, would be the names of all the guests attending, e.g. Mr. & Mrs. Lew Wasserman – 301. Once that had been accomplished all the cards would be alphabetized and in the "W's" you would find Mr. & Mrs. Lew Wasserman - 301. We would end up with some 700 cards strewn all over the floor of the office under each individual letter from A to Z and that information would then be transferred to what would become the finished seating book. At most fundraising dinners, as guests arrived they would check in at a desk and give their name to receive their table number. This often created a huge bottleneck and was not the best start to what was supposed to be a fun evening. Although incredibly time-consuming, the seating book became a very efficient method of giving the guests their table number without standing in line. As everyone showed a ticket to enter, a copy of the book was smoothly handed to them as they walked through to the cocktail area. Later on, it also allowed for great table-hopping and star–gazing and served as a great souvenir of the evening.

AFI's Tribute was a good example of this system in motion. The producer and director of the TV show with other members of the camera crew, together with executives from the corporate side, would come into my office and move their flags around. Sometimes there were major conflicts between the two, with one group moving their flags to a different table and then the others moving them back again. Somehow it worked itself out in the end, but not without major tension ensuing on many occasions.

Once, when Angela Lansbury was a celebrity guest, she approached me with the seating book in hand quite concerned that she couldn't find her table number as she had forgotten her glasses. The trouble was at that point, mine were in my evening purse, but between us with much squinting I managed to find it and off she went. Fortunately, the table numbers placed on each table were big enough to be read from quite a distance. I was never sure whether Miss Lansbury was recognized for who she was or rather as the fictional Jessica Fletcher she portrayed for many years in the television series *Murder She Wrote*.

In 1982, at the dinner honoring the great director Frank Capra, Jessica Lange came with renowned Russian ballet dancer Mikhail Baryshnikov as her date. She hadn't let us know the name of her guest, and I remember the head of AFI at that time coming up to me in great distress saying she had just seen Mikhail Baryshnikov but he couldn't possibly be there as "he didn't have a flag!" I think they all enjoyed the evening, though.

Some producers and directors, the occasional cinematographer, and set and costume designers become recognizable names, but very few tickets were sold from a movie box office based on who wrote the screenplay. Yet the writers play a pivotal role in the success of a film. It doesn't matter how talented the actors or how accomplished the director, without the right script, the project can turn into a complete disaster.

I very often felt more intimidated meeting writers than actors since they could usually articulate far better than I what they were talking about. On the other hand, some writers were very shy and didn't socialize well at all after being cooped up in their little rooms all day long, mostly alone with their projects.

On one occasion, when the foyer at Greystone was being used by the LA film critics for their annual awards presentation in January of 1977, I met two of the most well known writers of all time. Gore Vidal, probably best known for his novel *Myra Breckenridge,* but who had won an Oscar for his screenplay for *Ben Hur* in 1959 was one. The other was Paddy Chayefsky, whose award-winning screenplay giving a scathing, satirical look at the television industry *Network* won him one of his three

Academy Awards. The timing was ironic, for Peter Finch, whose ringing words "I'm as mad as hell and I'm not going to take it anymore!" made the film so famous, died just two days earlier. He was scheduled to be a featured speaker at a Screen Actors Guild seminar the following day, but alas it was not to be.

That Wednesday, January 19, 1977, was quite a day because as well as meeting these two distinguished writers, other fans included actor Robert De Niro of *Godfather* fame, comedienne Carol Burnett best known for her long running TV show, morning game show host Regis Philbin, and radio disc jockey Gary Owens, whose dulcet tones introduced "Rowan and Martin's Laugh In" every week.

* * * * *

In the 1970s and 1980s, one master of his craft, best known for producing and directing "disaster" movies, was Irwin Allen. Two of his most successful offerings were *The Poseidon Adventure* and *The Towering Inferno*, in which he dreamt up dreadful and ghastly scenarios of death and destruction and then proceeded to put them on film in a highly entertaining way. He was also a fanatic about how he was perceived in Hollywood. Along with other "behind the scenes" people, he was not recognizable to any degree, no matter how famous his films became. However, it was essential to him he was considered a major player at all times. The manager of the then supposedly best (and most expensive) restaurant in Los Angeles, Chasens, told me Irwin Allen had a favorite table and woe betide anyone else who was found seated there when Mr. Allen appeared (with or without a reservation). In those days, it was *the* restaurant to be seen dining in, and Allen had taken possession of a table right inside the door - the first one seen on entering, and the most visible. Without actually putting his name on it, it became common knowledge whose table it was so there was never any doubt who was seated there.

For over 20 years at AFI's Life Achievement Award Dinner, Allen insisted on having the same table – on the rail of the first level closest to the stage of the International Ballroom at the Beverly Hilton Hotel in Beverly Hills. Eventually, after his death when his wife Sheila still attended accompanied by the usual glittering guests, she maintained ownership of the same table. She was appalled one year when it had been given to someone else, and although seated right next to the original, Sheila and her company left the occasion before the festivities had begun. As far as I know, she never attended the event again.

In the happy days when the Allens were resident at Table 201, their guests almost always included comedian George Burns – with a variety of pretty young things on his arm and his cigar in full swing - the Borgnines with Tova looking younger every year and Ernie his usual cheerful and disarming self, the Caines, with Shakira always looking stunning and Michael smiling, affable and always charming.

* * * * *

A particularly well known "behind the scenes" director who was one of the exceptions to the rule of name recognition was Sir Alfred Hitchcock, whom I didn't meet until he was almost eighty years old. He was in a wheelchair and all shot up with cortisone when he accepted his Life Achievement Award in 1979. Despite his frail health preventing him from attending rehearsals, nothing stopped his inimitable sense of humor. Having been wheeled to the podium to receive his award on the evening of March 7, he slid the star statuette inside his jacket as if he was stealing it, still seated in the wheel chair with a thoroughly wicked grin on his face.

I don't remember a more diverse or cosmopolitan group than those assembled to honor Hitchcock on his special night. Dame Judith Anderson, two years his senior, was in the audience to cheer him on and represent celebrity input from around the world. Born in Adelaide, Australia, she was probably most remembered for playing Mrs. Danvers in Hitchcock's classic *Rebecca*, for which she was nominated for an Academy Award.

From every category of filmmaking, and another cosmopolitan group to say the least, the actors present included Swedish-born Ingrid Bergman, who had created a massive scandal by having an affair with married film director Roberto Rossellini back in the 1950s. No one would have turned a hair today, but she suffered enormously for it. She paid a warm tribute to Alfred Hitchcock, having been in three of his films. From UK, Michael Caine and Sean Connery were joined by Cary Grant (who was originally from England, having become a US citizen in 1942). Jimmy Stewart, Gene Wilder, William Shatner, Anne Bancroft and husband Mel Brooks, Mia Farrow, Joseph Cotton, Jane Wyman, Charlton Heston, Irene Dunne, the previous year's honoree Henry Fonda, television's prime-time drama *Dynasty* star John Forsythe, and actress turned animal rights activist Tippi Hedren, so famous for *The Birds*, all attended. Perhaps representing the most recognized and suspenseful Hitchcock movie, Janet Leigh of *Psycho* fame was there – who could ever forget the shower scene – together with Anthony Perkins, so memorable in the same film as Norman Bates.

Then there were his fellow directors – Canadian Arthur Hiller, from France François Truffaut, from the States Steven Spielberg, William Wyler, Franklin J. Schaffner, and Robert Wise. Screenwriter Tom Mankiewicz was at a table next to best selling author Michael

Crichton, and from the musical arena the songwriter lyricists Alan and Marilyn Bergman (responsible for classics like "The Windmills of Your Mind," "What Are You Doing The Rest of Your Life" and "The Way We Were") sat close to Barbara Streisand, Neil Diamond, and "I Am Woman" songstress Helen Reddy, not to mention "The Boss" himself, Bruce Springsteen, and conductor, arranger, and composer Quincy Jones. Funnymen Chevy Chase, Rich Little, Robin Williams, and Dom DeLuise, were joined by renowned costume designer Edith Head, who worked on no less than eleven Hitchcock films, *Playboy* founder Hugh Hefner, and from the political arena the current Mayor of Los Angeles, Tom Bradley.

It was truly an extraordinary gathering. If a bomb had been dropped on the Beverly Hilton Hotel that night, almost the entire film industry would have been wiped out. In fact, that almost happened at a later Tribute, but that's another story!

The *coup de grace* of this historic evening was the dessert. Each of the 120 tables was served an individual cheesecake with the famous Hitchcock profile etched in chocolate on each one. It must have taken the pastry chef hours to complete, but was thoroughly appreciated by all the guests, some of whom were truly loathe to have it cut up and served!

That same famous profile served as the cover of the evening's program book, which Hitchcock dutifully signed for me!

* * * * *

One of the best-loved films of all time seems to be *The Sound of Music*, starring Julie Andrews and Christopher Plummer.

The director of this classic, Robert Wise, had an amazing career, with his first nomination for an Academy Award coming in 1941 for editing *Citizen Kane*. But he is best known for his directing skills, having won awards for two all time greats - *West Side Story* and *The Sound of Music*. It made perfect sense then that in 1998, when AFI honored him, Julie Andrews should play host.

On that particular event, I worked closely with Bob's wife Millicent to make sure everything would be to his satisfaction. Milly, as she liked to be called, had met her husband when she was his nurse some years earlier. She was very English, charming in her way, but terribly protective and equally controlling – some would say downright bossy and difficult. I think she only tolerated me because I, too, was from England and she felt we understood each other. It's amazing what an English accent can do. Every time AFI and Millie disagreed on something, I would be thrown into the mix to sort it out. I got quite good at compatible solutions and keeping everybody happy.

Mr. Wise's evening brought forth a bevy of celebrities from all fields, including Charmian Carr who played Liesl in *The Sound of Music,* and Rita Moreno and George Chakiras from *West Side Story*. Also in the audience were Hollywood's top couple of the decade Warren Beatty and Annette Benning, a young George Clooney, Candace Bergen, Theodore Bikel, Ernest Borgnine, Red Buttons, Jack Lemmon and Felicia Farr, Karl Malden, Patricia Neal, Leonard Nimoy, William Shatner, Gregory Peck, and Tom Selleck looking like the beautiful people they all were dressed up in black tie and happy to party!

From the music scene, the Bergmans, Marvin Hamlisch, Melissa Manchester, former member of The "Monkees" Michael Nesmith, and Neil Sedaka were sprinkled in with entrepreneur and TV personality Merv Griffin. Former Rolling Stones advisor Prince Rupert zu Löwenstein was there as well as directors John Frankenheimer, Arthur Hiller, Dan Petrie, and Franklin Schaffner. With more than a thousand guests gracing the Beverly Hilton Hotel's Grand Ballroom, it was a truly spectacular evening.

* * * * *

One of the things I remember most about Steven Spielberg was that he had the nicest people working for him. The movie business is notoriously cutthroat, and this can create tension on all levels, from secretaries to executive producers. So it was to Mr. Spielberg's great credit that his team seemed to be an exception to that rule. You could always tell when the boss was nasty or nice by the initial treatment received from the outer office. At his headquarters, I was very impressed with all the awards and trophies displayed everywhere acknowledging his amazing accomplishments, although he himself was unassuming and quite down to earth.

In 1995, AFI presented him with the 23rd Life Achievement Award, and what a star-studded event that was! Hosted by Tom Hanks, the entire evening was elegant and sophisticated. With fellow director George Lucas so famous for creating *Star Wars* and studio executive Sid Sheinberg seated at the head table, Spielberg was in good company. Mr. Sheinberg is credited with discovering Steven Spielberg in 1973 when working under Lew Wasserman at Universal Studios, who was also in the audience that evening, and the rest as they say, is history. Steven directed some of the highest-grossing films of all time.

* * * * *

William Wyler was not only one of the most talented directors of his time, winning Oscars for *Mrs. Miniver* in 1942, *The Best Years of Our Lives* in 1946, and *Ben-Hur* in 1959, but a charming gentleman of the old school. He and his wife Tally were strong supporters of AFI and attended several events held at Greystone Mansion when the Institute was housed there.

Mr. Wyler was one of the earliest recipients of AFI's Life Achievement Award. On March 9, 1976, at the Century Plaza Hotel in Los Angeles, he was fêted by the film industry's greats. There were quite a few problems "behind the scenes" as well as in front of the house that year, but only a few guests, including the Wylers, seemed to notice, though editing for the television show to be aired later took on a whole new meaning! At that time a volunteer was handling the dinner seating, and I was more of a production assistant on the television show. Due to unforeseen personal problems, the individual concerned was not able to accomplish her task and the whole thing became a major disaster when she actually left out an entire table of guests, all of whom marched out in high dudgeon and had to be placated later. Fortunately, I had nothing to do with it that year.

For some reason, the film clips were misplaced and the work print had to be used, causing major concern for the producer and director. The attendant guests were none the wiser, but I think heads rolled over the next few days. The following year, I was put in charge of the seating and dinner arrangements.

Some years later, in January 1981 after AFI had moved from Greystone Mansion to Immaculate Heart College in Hollywood, William and Tally Wyler were among the guests attending a celebratory dinner party. Other guests that evening included John Gavin, who later that year would become United States Ambassador to Mexico but was probably best remembered for his acting roles opposite stars like Doris Day in *Midnight Lace*. Actors Charlton Heston and Tony Bill, along with

"*Hollywood Reporter*" columnist George Christy, also graced the dinner tables with other notables from various related businesses.

I was sitting next to Mr. Wyler at this dinner, and on a printed card explaining the purpose of the event quite unsolicited he wrote "To Jackie Frame – a *Girl for All Seasons.*" another lovely memento for my book of memories!

* * * * *

Billy Wilder had to be one of the most versatile filmmakers of the 20th century. He received Academy Award nominations for directing, producing, and writing, winning in all those categories for *The Apartment,* starring Jack Lemmon and Shirley MacLaine. Together with Martin Scorsese, he is the most nominated director in the history of the Academy Awards.

In 1986 he collected AFI's prestigious award, and I remember him being rather jolly on the phone although his thick accent (he was born in Sucha Beskidzka, Austria-Hungary, now Poland, and spent some years in Germany before World War II), sometimes made him a little difficult to understand.

His Tribute Dinner was a complete sell-out. We had the longest wait list I could remember. Hysterical phone calls from secretaries and junior executives alike begged for a table, promising that the callers would lose their jobs if their bosses couldn't attend.

The evening was an unqualified success made all the more memorable the following morning when Mr. Wilder called and asked, quite deservedly and sounding highly delighted with himself, "Vee ver a hit?" Of course, when you have directed films like *Ninotchka, The Lost Weekend, Double Indemnity, Sunset Boulevard* and *Some Like It Hot*, it's difficult not to be a hit, so it was a statement really, not a question.

Despite having directed some major dramas Billy Wilder was best remembered for his comedies, so it was ironic he should die on the same day as two other legendary funny men – Milton Berle and Dudley Moore – on March 27, 2002. They say everything happens in threes.

* * * * *

During a span of 23 years in my role as Dinner Coordinator for AFI's Tributes, there was only one honoree who wrote notes to his friends and colleagues both before and after the dinner: Frank Capra.

In November 1981, I was asked to spend some time with him writing letters of invitation he personally wanted to send. Mr. Capra was living in La Quinta, a quaint little desert enclave some twenty miles east of Palm Springs. I drove down one morning and spent the afternoon working on the letters. Later I had dinner with him alone because Mrs. Capra was suffering from emphysema. It was wonderful to listen to Capra talk about his early days in the 1930s and 1940s, when things were so different, and also to hear of his activities during World War II.

One of the most brilliant directors of his time, Frank Capra's films became classics. Starting in 1934 with *It Happened One Night*, starring Claudette Colbert and Clark Gable, he followed up with Ronald Colman and Jane Wyatt in *Lost Horizon*. *Arsenic and Old Lace* came next, with a wickedly irresistible Cary Grant, and then the ever popular *It's A Wonderful Life*. An emotional James Stewart realizing what life would have been like if he had not been born to save the day made for timeless storytelling. The film still screens regularly every Christmas and never gets old. This was just the beginning - there were many others in between along, with innumerable awards and accolades over the years.

When Mr. Capra returned to the desert after the event, he again wrote personal thank you notes to everyone who had been part of the show. I returned to La Quinta to type them for him. Each one was special and different, and he took a lot of time and trouble over them. He also told me lots of stories about World War II, when at the peak of his career, he directed eleven war documentaries for the U.S. government's *Why We Fight* series, winning an Academy Award for one and a Distinguished Service Medal when the war ended.

He added the story of how after being presented with an honorary OBE (Order of the British Empire) by Sir Winston Churchill, he and the great orator became very good friends. This contrasted starkly with some of the other incidents about how he got into trouble from time to time while serving in the US Army in Hawaii.

He also signed the first page of the program book covering his award night – *"To Jackie Frame a wondrous name for a wondrous dame – Frank Capra."*

In 2014 I returned to La Quinta Resort and Club, now a Waldorf Astoria resort, and was so pleased to see that there is now a meeting room with Capra's name above the door and a plaque commemorating his life's work. They are very proud of him there, and I think he remains La Quinta's most celebrated resident.

* * * * *

And then there were the Volunteer committees! Their names could be an essential element to any major event because they added prestige to the evening. Usually the wives of studio executives some were wonderful while others did nothing, but they all loved to see who else was on the list.

One of the best was Nancy Olson Livingston. *Sunset Boulevard,* one of the most enduring films of all time, gave Nancy Olson probably one of the greatest moments of her career. Gloria Swanson and William

Holden were classic in their portrayals of the aging former movie star and the struggling young screenwriter who inadvertently ends up at her dilapidated mansion on Sunset Boulevard when his car breaks down. Playing the role of William Holden's girlfriend, Nancy was nominated for Best Supporting Actress and kept her Oscar nomination certificate framed for posterity in her guest bathroom. I know that because I was in her home (and the guest bathroom) several times over the years as Nancy, one of the most elegant ladies among the Beverly Hills hierarchy, was one of the most supportive members of Los Angeles society and served on any number of committees for events I was handling.

After pretty much giving up her acting career by the 1970s, she and Capitol Records President Alan Livingston were living happily ever after in Beverly Hills. Nancy remained extremely active, however, volunteering her services to different organizations (she was reputedly incapable of saying no, a statement she readily acknowledged as absolutely true) and it was when she co-chaired AFI's Tribute to Alfred Hitchcock in 1979 that I first met her. Not only was she always a pleasure to be around, but Nancy would work tirelessly on each project. She was definitely one of the exceptions to the rule as far as making a major contribution to the success of the event. I would get rather cross with many Ladies Committee volunteers who attended meetings, did absolutely nothing to help, and then basked in the glory of having their name on the invitations. Not Nancy, though: she was a real trooper, as well as the essence of calm, and certainly never made a scene, even under the most difficult of circumstances. In fact she would quite quietly always get her own way with charm and diplomacy. Some said she should have been a politician. If only there had been more like her!

Chapter Eight

So what was it like "Behind the Scenes?" Traumatic, pressured, exciting, unique, harrowing, stimulating, boring, memorable, forgettable, disappointing, exhilarating, impressive, creative ... you name it – they all apply, but most of all it was history in the making, at least for me!

Chapter Nine: Togetherness

There are many famous show business families on both sides of the pond. Known in both the UK and the US, among the most prominent are the Redgraves. Beginning in the London theatre with Sir Michael, father of Oscar, Tony, Golden Globe and Emmy award winner Vanessa, and her siblings Lynn and Corin. The next generation included Vanessa's daughters Natasha and Joely Richardson, as well as Corin's daughter Jemma to complete an impressive dynasty.

I encountered Lynn at a fundraising dinner that I was helping to coordinate. She caused a potentially chaotic situation by bringing extra guests that she thought we could squeeze into her table if they didn't mind being a bit cozy. She didn't mean to cause chaos, but equally she didn't know about the Beverly Hills Fire Department and its codes.

Celebrities can't help it! For the most part they think there is one set of rules for them and another for ordinary members of the public like us. That doesn't mean they aren't lovely and charming – it's just they can't help themselves when put in certain surroundings. Never was that more true than with Lynn Redgrave, who had been given two complimentary tickets to attend the Tribute Dinner honoring Dustin Hoffman in 1999. Being generous of heart and thinking it wouldn't make any difference, she decided to invite two additional friends to accompany her and her escort. When I was called to solve a problem at her table because there were fourteen people there and only twelve chairs, I had no clue who the extra couple were so had to do a roll call. That was embarrassing to say the least, but when it turned out that Lynn's friends were the culprits, it was even more embarrassing for her. "Oh Jackie," she said, "I'm sure no one would mind if we got cozy and added two more chairs." While it was already cozy with twelve, fourteen was not physically possible. That wasn't the major stumbling block. I knew full well that if the Beverly Hills Fire Department got wind of it, the whole event would be shut down, and that was most definitely not an option! As diplomatically as possible, I explained that it wasn't up to me, it was a Fire Department ruling but that if the extra couple would attend, I would find them somewhere else to sit. This is all taking place, I might add, just minutes before the honoree was due to make his entrance and be photographed winding his way between tables, thus creating the opening shot for the television special. Lynn was in camera range, and the last thing I wanted was to be seen overseeing guests at a problem table as part of the beginning of the show! Mercifully, despite her pleas that they stay, the extra couple followed me and I went to my Plan B book, where I had a list of people who had not collected their tickets and were considered "no shows." This just goes to show how essential it is to have a Plan B, C, D and E for every possible set of circumstances! True to form, though, the situation did not prevent Lynn from being a charming and delightful person.

     Vanessa being the most famous member of the family, I was interested to read in a recent biography that she and I have something in common. We both received the same amount of money in our first pay packets, albeit in different years – she in her first theatre outing, mine at the BBC, in the magnificent amount of 7 pounds sterling (about $10). A long time ago for both of us!

Chapter Nine

* * * * *

Another illustrious show business family to emanate from England was that of John Mills.

Knighted by the Queen in 1960, Sir John Mills, CBE appeared in more than 120 films spanning seventy years and lived to the ripe old age of 97! He received an Academy Award for Best Supporting Actor for his work in David Lean's epic *Ryan's Daughter*, and it was due to that association he was invited to attend the American Film Institute's Life Achievement Award Tribute to Sir David on March 8, 1990.

He came with both of his famous daughters, Hayley and Juliet, as well as other members of the family. Hayley had become a child star in the US appearing in *Pollyanna*, *The Parent Trap*, and *Whistle Down the Wind* in the 1960s while Juliet followed suit, making a name for herself as the star of television's *Nanny and the Professor*. The Mills family continued their trait of being surrounded by celebrities not only that evening but in real life with Hayley's godmother being actress Vivien Leigh and her godfather, Noël Coward.

Talking with Hayley that evening, it was evident that they were a happy and proud family, all enjoying their lives despite the inevitable ups and downs associated with show business. Both sisters had caused ripples of criticism by their marriages, Hayley to a much older Roy Boulting in 1971, and Juliet to a much younger Maxwell Caulfield in 1980.

A classic example of the downside to life in the theatre was a play in London called *The Lizard on the Rock*, which played for just a few days in May 1963. Juliet starred in it, but it's not even mentioned in her biographical material as it was a flop and closed very shortly after it opened. I remember thinking how dreadfully disappointing it must be to learn all those lines and perfect a performance only to be allowed to play it once or twice.

* * * * *

American families have equal claims to fame!

Let's start with the Fondas.

In all the years of coordinating AFI's Life Achievement Award Dinner, only one recipient sent me a hand written thank you letter. I never expected any kind of acknowledgement since my role was very much behind the scenes, and most people attending had no clue I even existed. I took that as a compliment, because it meant there were no huge glitches from my end. With everything going so smoothly, there was surely no need for a professional to coordinate activities. Guests would have their cars valet parked, walk through the entrance, receive a seating chart giving them their table numbers, be seated, have drinks and dinner, and enjoy a show. Why on earth would someone be required to put that together? Of course, as anyone who has had anything to do with the details of an organized event knows – be they a volunteer or paid professional, - there are many details involved.

It was after Henry Fonda's event in 1978 that I was thrilled, surprised, and very appreciative of his thoughtful letter thanking me for helping to make his experience that evening so pleasurable. In his acceptance speech, he admitted to being very shy and only really feeling at ease when playing the part of someone else, which is why he became an actor. That night, having to play the role of himself, he was not comfortable. His acceptance speech showed that he was visibly nervous. Nevertheless, he was most gracious and surrounded by generations of family at the head table, including wife Shirlee together with Jane,

Bridget, Peter, Amy, and Justin, definitely enhanced his evening and made him feel more at home.

Famous daughter Jane was (and still is) a law unto herself. I met her at the evening honoring her father in 1978, when she was married to Tom Hayden. I remember having to give her a message from her husband the afternoon of the dinner and going to her suite in the Beverly Hilton Hotel to deliver it personally. I was so used to addressing all the celebrities by their first names, I foolishly did the same to her, which she did not appreciate one bit and quite rightly chastised me. Of course, I had no idea what was in the message, but she didn't seem too happy to receive it.

However, Jane's most memorable moment for me came when she hosted the Barbara Stanwyck Tribute in 1987. Fortunately, the show didn't go out live because the first words out of her mouth as she began her introduction naming the honoree before the star-studded audience were "I have always been a great admirer of Barbara Streisand!" With a mortified gasp when she realized what she had said, she clasped her hand to her mouth, wheeled around and took a few steps back before returning to the podium to start again.

At the end of the show, when all the guests had left the ballroom, another introduction was taped and editing would do the rest, so to this day the only people who heard her *faux pas* were 1,200 of Hollywood's finest.

* * * * *

And then there are the Douglases.

Here's another prominent family, whose name has been recognizable for decades. Headed by Kirk and followed by his equally famous son Michael, I hadn't had occasion to get to know either until

Kirk was honored by AFI with the Life Achievement Award in 1991. Even then, it wasn't Kirk who was most visible, but his wife, Anne. She and I had far more discussions about how the evening would evolve. Kirk would do as he was told she said.

One of the most memorable events surrounding this Hollywood legend occurred just before he received his award in March. A month earlier, he had survived a helicopter crash in which two people died. I think that was as close as we ever came to losing an honoree before the Tribute Diner.

On his special evening he was surrounded by family and friends where guests who paid their respects and told personal stories, included Alan Alda, Lauren Bacall, Robert Wagner, Henry Winkler, Red Buttons, James Coburn, Don Rickles, Shirley MacLaine, and Gregory Peck.

*****

Although not necessarily family, or even related, other couplings caused memorable occasions to say the least.

One such event occurred in 2004 at a private home in Santa Barbara, California where John Cleese of *Monty Python* fame and Julia Child, cooking genius and author of *Mastering the Art of French Cooking* were found together in the spotlight.

At that time, I was working with a non-profit group affiliated with the International Women's Forum in Washington, DC. The members of this illustrious group would meet each month for a special event. I handled the administration of all the business meetings and social gatherings throughout the year. An annual event always included a Weekend Retreat of seminars, discussion groups, and socializing. In 2004, it took place in Santa Barbara, a delightful and very affluent beach community about a hundred miles north of Los Angeles.

Chapter Nine

Saturday evening's program included a visit from Julia Child, renowned cookbook author and host of the first live television show to feature cooking, *The French Chef,* which initially aired in 1963. The story of her life was told again in the 2009 film *Julie & Julia,* based on a cooking blog by a New York home cook, Julie Powell, who set upon the task of cooking all of Julia Child's meals over the course of a year. A neighbor and good friend of our hostess, Julia was 91 and in a wheel chair, but that didn't prevent her from thoroughly enjoying the party. She constantly toasted everyone with the famous glass of red wine prominent in her right hand.

The other speaker for the evening was an American psychotherapist, John Cleese's wife Alyce Faye Cleese. She had written a book about the seemingly inevitable roller-coaster "mother/daughter" relationship.

Mrs. John Cleese came with her husband, and to be truthful most of us were much more interested in meeting him, although we had been warned that in general conversation he would not be funny, nor did he like small talk. We were a little intimidated to say the least, as he is a very imposing figure, being extremely tall. He was also the only man in a room full of about 65 women so he was approached with some trepidation.

One member of the group had a fashion line of custom designed knitwear. She and I were discussing some of her new ideas when we noticed Mr. Cleese looking rather disinterested in his current conversation, so we decided to go over and rescue him. Here again the Brit in all of us immediately provided a communication link to our conversation (the knitting lady came from the north of England). It turned out, indeed, that he was not funny, but we had a most interesting chat about knitting which he professed to appreciate. We discussed men's sweaters at length, as he had ideas about a custom line to include his initials. Nothing ever came of it, but I couldn't help thinking that somewhere along the line there had to be a Monty Python sketch that included Mr. Cleese knitting.

* * * * *

Two names forever intertwined were Paul Newman and Joanne Woodward.

I feel as if I have had Paul Newman around the house as long as I can remember. Of course, I am referring to his salad dressings and various other culinary delights, as every time I open the fridge door there he is. The real thing was much better, needless to say, and who wasn't utterly captivated by those incredibly blue eyes and such a handsome face?

When I met him, he was a little preoccupied so I got the briefest of smiles but Joanne was charming and friendly. Prior to this introduction and some months earlier, when I was handling a fundraising auction of gifts from celebrities, Joanne had donated a handmade needlepoint pillow, and this was the perfect opportunity to thank her for such a personal and truly lovely gift.

It was Friday, March 30, 1979, and the closing night of FILMEX, an annual film festival held in Los Angeles in those days. Laurence Olivier was to receive an award presented by Gregory Peck.

The evening had started with a screening of his latest film, *A Little Romance,* which was to be followed by a champagne reception. One of Olivier's earliest films, *Rebecca,* had also become one of the most memorable. It so happened an original screen test had been found showing a young Vivien Leigh (then Mrs. Olivier) auditioning for the role of the second "Mrs. de Winter." It was shown after the main feature, and word had it she was much too pretty for the role so it went to Joan Fontaine, Olivia de Havilland's sister, who won an Academy Award nomination for her performance.

Despite his prominence in the theatre and extraordinary portrayals of Shakespearian characters, to me Laurence Olivier would always be Heathcliff in *Wuthering Heights,* directed by William Wyler in the film that brought him to the notice of the American audience.

But back to the FILMEX party. Olivier made a grand entrance accompanied by Robert Wagner and Natalie Wood, and that was when my first introduction came about. It was rather unusual in a number of ways. The star of the evening, he was seated on a couch surrounded by wellwishers, and I was standing behind it so that in order to shake my hand he had to twist his arm backwards to grasp it. That didn't prevent him from doing so with his usual vim and vigor so much so I could feel a ring I was wearing which housed a substantial amethyst stone digging into the finger in question and becoming extremely painful. I didn't care, though, I was shaking the hand of Laurence Olivier so I just let him hang on for as long as possible.

I didn't always appreciate Olivier's work, though, particularly in the directing department. In February 1970, he held the reins for Maggie Smith in a production of one of my favorite plays, *Three Sisters* by Anton Chekhov. But here I did not like the way it was presented and even found Maggie Smith's voice very irritating. I fell asleep in the third Act and found the evening disappointing and expensive.

Also at this star studded event was Dudley Moore. I was reminded again of the first time I saw him and ended up in floods of tears I was laughing so hard. It was at a performance of *Beyond the Fringe*, the brilliantly funny satirical review starring Peter Cook, Dudley Moore, Alan Bennett, and Jonathan Miller. It was 1962, and I was sitting in the front row of the upper circle of the Fortune Theatre in London experiencing British comedy at its awe-inspiring best!

Started in combination with the Cambridge Footlights and the Oxford Revue in 1960, *Beyond the Fringe* was the forerunner to British television's highly successful topical political satire, poking fun with highly irreverent humor at the events of the past week with *That Was the Week That Was.* Introduced by the wonderful Sir David Frost, the opening number was always a highlight with Millicent Martin's amazing rendition in song of the details of all topics in the news from the past week.

Another memorable collaboration came later when Dudley Moore and Peter Cook teamed up again for a *Saturday Night Live* appearance and performed their classic skit, *One Leg Too Few*, which aired in 1976. Peter Cook played a theatrical producer auditioning a one-legged man (played by Dudley Moore) for the part of *Tarzan* culminating in the classic line "I've got nothing against your right leg, Mr. Spiggot. The trouble is neither have you."

At the FILMEX party, I was in a group surrounding Mr. Moore. We were all chatting and laughing – you couldn't ever do anything but laugh around him – but on this occasion I managed not to cry.

Chapter Ten:
Difficult Challenges

The most difficult situations were usually caused by celebrities who were less confident and whose careers weren't necessarily going forward, but rather slipping behind. This inevitably caused a feeling of acute anxiety, which can manifest in a hostile attitude. That's a round about way of saying, they felt it necessary to put everyone else down and play a great deal of one-upmanship before somebody else did the same to them!

Never was this more evident than in the case of Bette Davis, who came across as a different person every time I met her.

My most definitive recollection of her brings to mind the words "bitter," "meanspirited," and "rude." I believe she was very unhappy, but she had survived the most difficult times, particularly in the early part of her career, under contract to the infamous studio head Jack Warner. That could well have influenced her personality from then on.

From the very beginning, things started on the wrong foot. When she arrived in Hollywood, the studio representative who went to meet her train reportedly left without her because he couldn't find anyone who looked like a movie star.

At AFI's Life Achievement Award in 1982, when director Frank Capra was honored, Bette was invited to sit at head table with him because she was one of the stars of *Pocketful of Miracles* from 1961. It was widely known Miss Davis was a chain smoker, but in those days nobody paid a lot of attention to that habit. However, on this particular occasion, because Mrs. Capra was suffering from emphysema and might have needed oxygen, there was to be no smoking in that area.

"Bette," pleaded the producer of the show, "you cannot smoke with an oxygen tank under the table."

"That's not my problem," she retorted tartly. "If Mrs. Capra might have needed oxygen, then maybe you should seat her at another table because I couldn't possibly go without a cigarette."

In the end, she did sit with the Capras at the head table with the other celebrities, but disappeared on several occasions to go to the ladies' room or outside into the lobby to have a cigarette. That left an empty chair, which, when shots of the honoree were cut into the television show, caused great annoyance and unnecessary difficulties for the editor.

On another occasion, when she attended the same event as a guest (all the past honorees were given two complimentary tickets to the subsequent tributes), her secretary came with her because it seemed all her friends had deserted her by then and she couldn't find anyone else! She was in her seventies at that time. As her epitaph reads, "She did it the hard way." By then it really showed.

Once I remember she was sitting alone at a reception so I went over to say hello and opened with "how nice that you could come," to which she replied tartly "Well, you can tell I came because I'm sitting here, aren't I," at which point she indicated in no uncertain terms our conversation was over! She remained sitting alone.

* * * * *

Another challenging client came in the form of broadcast journalist, author, and television superwoman Barbara Walters.

Chapter Ten

The first time we met was in New York on Saturday, September 21, 1986, at a meeting held in her Park Avenue apartment. My party planning genius friend Clive David and I had been retained to coordinate a reception celebrating her recent marriage to Merv Adelson. There were to be two such parties, one on the West Coast and this one on the East Coast, to be held at the Pierre Hotel later that month.

Barbara was not the easiest person to work with. I think she only tolerated me because she had a daughter with the same name, Jackie! I found her personality in complete contrast to the image portrayed on the television screen, but that is probably true of many celebrities.

One of the problems when working with a perfectionist is just that – they are perfectionists. Barbara Walters proved it to herself and everyone else every day. In addition to being an extremely high-powered professional, she led an extraordinarily disciplined life, with every minute of the day planned and accounted for.

I remember that at one very late-night meeting, it was decided to cancel a meeting planned for early the following morning. Barbara went into a blind panic at the thought of having a thirty-minute gap in her schedule where she wouldn't have anything to do. A decision was made to proceed with the meeting as scheduled.

Earlier, after Clive and I had just arrived in New York, we had a meeting with the happy couple. Because of her very busy and highly organized schedule, we didn't start until late in the evening. It was fortunate that I was on Pacific time as we didn't finish until after 1am. It wasn't what you would call a particularly peaceable exchange of ideas, either, as both principals involved seemed to feel they would get their own way based on the volume of their verbal abuse. Neither listened to the other, and in the end we were all emotionally drained. Although apologies were forthcoming all around, I was totally exhausted and seriously wondered what I had to look forward to over the next few days.

At one point I wrote this in my diary:

"Barbara Walters is driving Clive up the wall, down the other side, and back again! He's tearing his hair out in frustration, she's being impossible. She seems to relish putting people down, will not listen and can be thoroughly rude."

On another occasion, there were about eight of us in the ballroom of the Pierre working out table locations and seating when Barbara and Merv disagreed violently over something. In true dramatic fashion Barbara turned to her audience, the group witnessing the screaming match, and said, "Don't look so shocked, that's what husbands are for!"

Prior to the party, Clive had worked tirelessly with the florist on every detail of the blooms and blossoms that would decorate the room, and it was a massive order. After everything had been confirmed and paid for (by Clive), Barbara saw a photograph of an all white-themed room and insisted the decor be changed accordingly. She wouldn't take no for an answer and it wasn't until Clive finally broke down in tears that the issue was resolved and the original plan stayed in place.

The actual party was a success for the guests, but a nightmare for all behind the scenes. Up until 4 o'clock Barbara was re-arranging the seating and moving people around from table to table. How the calligrapher and I managed to get the place cards in the right places by the time guests entered I do not know. Here again, my diary records, *"Ellen and I were hard pressed to get the cards out in time, but did because we are brilliant! I seriously doubt anyone else could have done it and I hope I never have to do it like that again."*

All in all, I think it was certainly one of the most challenging events I experienced. However, they couldn't all be wine and roses and lessons were learned, so it wasn't a total loss. But there was still the West Coast celebration to deal with.

In April 1987 a second and equally elaborate celebration was held at La Costa Spa north of La Jolla, most famous for a big ladies' tennis tournament that took place there every year. I commented that the place was run like a leaky faucet, with incompetent and unhelpful staff. Life didn't get any easier when Barbara and Merv arrived. It seemed they felt all the early plans (which they had made) should be changed, venues switched, menus discarded for alternate dishes and so on. However, here again the guests had a great time, particularly as the two-day event culminated in hot air balloons taking off into the wild blue yonder and, in one instance, almost never to be seen again. Apparently, the wind blew one of the balloons way off course and it was hours later found in a field some distance away.

* * * * *

Other challenging moments came from actor Glenn Ford, who seemed to take a delight in being demanding and difficult. Quite possibly the reason for his somewhat domineering attitude was because he wanted to impress his new and very pretty young bride, Cynthia.

Ford was invited to take part in AFI's second fundraising film cruise in the Caribbean. From the very beginning he wanted the virtually impossible. First, he said he and Cynthia couldn't possibly embark at all unless there was a two-bedroom, two-bathroom suite on board. At this time, he was 62 and Cynthia was 30, so I think she was actually calling the shots on this arrangement. As it turned out however, there was such a cabin on the Viking ship we were using, so it was duly booked despite the high costs.

The next trauma came when, upon landing from Los Angeles in Miami, I ushered the group into the taxi queue to take us to the hotel where we would overnight prior to the ship's departure next day. Mr. Ford considered himself way above getting into a taxi and shouted at me demanding a limousine, which he assured me in no uncertain terms, and in an equally loud voice was his accustomed mode of transportation. Needless to say, our budget did not run to such additional luxuries. He stamped his foot on the pavement in fury, but since it was very apparent there was no limo, nor was one likely to mysteriously appear, it was all a waste of time and he really had no choice but albeit begrudgingly to get into a cab.

Once aboard, the suite was to his, and probably more important at this time to Cynthia's, liking. He became more reasonable and even quite funny. A lighter note was struck at dinner one evening when he told the story of how he and Cynthia had met, saying he had had to decide whether to marry or adopt her!

* * * * *

Seating could always cause traumas. Generally speaking, a fundraising dinner takes place in the ballroom of a major hotel and can comprise as many as 150 tables of 10 or 12 guests. Needless to say, the table locations vary from very good to those referred to as "the back of the bus." When it comes to egos, the film and television industry takes first place, with studio heads and celebrities alike vying for the best. The studios have the funds to take the best places, but the celebrities have the visibility so both are equally important.

A good example of this tension came in March 1995 at the American Film Institute's Tribute to Steven Spielberg, which Faye Dunaway attended. She was the guest of an executive who had bought an entire table for ten. Although this gave him some priority as far as placement was concerned, it did not put him in camera range. He had invited nine people to be seated with him, and Faye was one of them. Being a big star, she felt she should be seated with the other celebrities in areas much closer to the stage. What she failed to understand was that because the table had been purchased in its entirety, one individual could not be plucked from it. She found me and said in no uncertain terms that something had to be done about it. She added equally firmly that she would feel obliged to walk out if no other place could be found. Eventually, she was obliged to return to her host but it was not with a good grace and whether she enjoyed the show or not I never knew.

* * * * *

Jack Lemmon caused one of the most embarrassing moments I ever had – but he didn't mean to. He was one of the most enduring and endearing celebrities I ever met, and the last thing he would knowingly do would be to create a scene or be difficult. His story is totally understandable, but didn't prevent a big problem!

In 1988 he was AFI's honoree and enjoyed an evening of accolades and anecdotes from colleagues such as Walter Matthau, Tony Curtis, and Shirley MacLaine.

However, it was at an earlier AFI celebration he created the most "challenging" moment for me. You might wonder why the usually mild mannered polite and very charming Mr. Lemmon would be seen gesticulating wildly in great distress and angrily demanding that a major star be removed from the table at which he was seated.

Here's what happened. As a regular attendee at AFI's galas and a good friend of George Stevens, Jr. (the founder of the American Film Institute and producer of the Life Achievement Award Tributes), Jack usually sat at one of George's tables. George had two particularly prominent tables, well within camera range, ensuring candid shots of the stars seated there throughout the show. This meant that specific seats were allocated to the celebrities in anticipation of their reactions and, we hoped, enthusiastic responses throughout the show.

In 1981, at the evening for Fred Astaire, Jack planned to attend with his perennial costar Walter Matthau and their wives Felicia and Carol (the couples were good friends and neighbors). Complimentary tickets to former honorees and celebrities were usually hand delivered, and in this instance they had all gone to the Lemmons. On this particular evening, the four of them were all to be seated together at one of George's tables. During the days prior to the tribute, Walter fell on the set of the picture he was making and broke his leg. Needless to say, that meant he would not be attending this particular tribute. Appropriate alternate celebrities were therefore added to the table taking the seats, which would have been occupied by the Matthaus.

On the night in question, I was hovering at the back of the ballroom ready to cope with inevitably angry people who didn't think they were seated at a good enough table when an equally enraged Jack Lemmon emerged from the throng of 1,200 guests to tell me his table was full and there weren't enough seats to accommodate everyone. Apparently he had decided to give the two tickets allotted to the Matthau's to another couple, as it seemed a waste not to use them. It never occurred to him that because Walter wouldn't be there other celebrities would be put in their place. It never occurred to us he would take it upon himself to give them away, either.

When I explained that alternate stars had been seated in place of the Matthaus, Jack became even more annoyed (I suspect he was very embarrassed over the misunderstanding and felt rather foolish) and said that the stars would just have to move so his friends and he could stay together.

At this point I should add that these tribute dinners were always completely sold out, and that every table in the room was filled to capacity. Per Fire Department codes, we were not permitted to squeeze more chairs around a table, even if the other guests didn't mind. In my calmest English accent, I explained that although they absolutely could not sit together, I would find a spot for his friends. My plan B immediately came into play (again), which was to go through the unclaimed tickets to see who had not shown up. I told Mr. Lemmon to send his friends to me so that I could take care of them. Having retrieved two unclaimed tickets from the will call box, and praying they would remain no shows, I took the couple to a table that was not in a comparable location. But was the best I could do.

After Jack's own tribute, he obviously didn't hold a grudge as he wrote me a charming thank you note before departing for a golf tournament in which he said how appreciative he was for all the hard work done, and acknowledging what a difficult chore it was to organize the seating.

* * * * *

Then there were the challenges brought forth from couples in the form of "the other halves." Two such ladies created potential turmoil.

Mrs. Anthony Quinn was a prima donna of the first degree! When her husband was a special guest at the head table for one of AFI's Salutes, she insisted they not be separated. Not able to cope with sitting anywhere but by his side, Yolanda demanded that we make room for her. Of course, that was not possible, for the head table guests were all associates of the honoree. But consideration could be given to the spouses or partners who were to be seated all together at a table in very close proximity. Yolanda would have none of that and stood behind her husband's chair at the head table refusing to move. The producer of the show saw what was happening and came in my direction to help (I thought). But he just sidled past and out of the corner of his mouth muttered, "Handle it, Jackie." I then very quietly but firmly and in my most calm of English accents (again), informed Mrs. Quinn she could either take her seat at the adjacent table or we would understand completely if she chose to miss the show and preferred to watch television in the suite provided upstairs in the hotel. She sat down at the adjacent table with the others.

One of the most prominent columnists in Hollywood for the last half of the 20th century was Army Archerd. His column in *Daily Variety* covered all the major celebrity events, of which there were many, and he was widely respected among his colleagues. However, his "other half" Selma was not. She became notorious for making scene after scene at events if she didn't get what she considered to be an "appropriate" table to suit their status. It mattered not to her that she personally had no status at all – it was her husband who was the famous writer, -- nor that they, as members of the press, never paid the vast sums often required for a ticket. She was Mrs. Army Archerd, and as such she felt she was show business royalty.

One of her more spectacular scenes came when she collared me to declare the table not to her liking. I explained that at this late stage moving her to another location would not improve the situation but that was not what she wanted to hear. Stamping her foot in rage, she started screaming that she hadn't paid extraordinary sums of money to have her hair done to be dumped in the back of the bus. It seemed the entire ballroom became privy to this statement, and people started to stare as she continued her tirade. There was nothing further I could do so I left her to it. She became a laughing stock and I truly wonder if she ever realized it.

Chapter Eleven:
Close Encounters

Every individual meeting with a celebrity brought forth an interesting and unique memory, but when there was more than one encounter, it became really special.

A perfect example of that was Gregory Peck.

Well, who hasn't swooned at the sound of Gregory Peck's mellifluous tones? He had one of the most beautiful speaking voices in the world, and I experienced it on my very first day in the office at The American Film Institute on November 11, 1974. My title was Assistant to the West Coast Director, who was then noted producer Martin Manulis, (*Days of Wine and Roses*), but in fact I was just a glorified secretary. Shortly after taking my place at a desk in the window of a beautiful room in Greystone Mansion, Beverly Hills, the home of AFI West, the phone rang. I dutifully picked it up and said "Martin Manulis' office." The voice at the other end said, "Greg Peck here, is he there?" I nearly fell off my chair, as I explained no he wasn't but could I take a message! That was the first of many encounters with one of Hollywood's greatest legends and most perfect gentleman.

On my third day, an important meeting took place with various senior staff members present. George Stevens, Jr., who founded The American Film Institute, was in town, from Washington DC, home to the east coast operation in the Kennedy Center. I was preparing some iced water to be taken into the meeting when George introduced me to

Charlton Heston. I remember being quite tongue tied and feeling as if I were in a scene from the *Mary Tyler Moore Show* as I tried to complete my task and shake hands at the same time. The celebrity intake continued, as also present were director George Roy Hill, best known for *Butch Cassidy and the Sundance Kid* as well as *The Sting*, and producer Walter Mirisch, who had won an Academy Award for Best Picture as producer of *In the Heat of the Night*, both Hollywood heavyweights! It was quite a week.

Gregory Peck was a staunch lifelong supporter of the arts and served on AFI's Board of Trustees. He began his career in the theater and founded the La Jolla Playhouse near San Diego in 1947. Perhaps his most famous role was that of Atticus Finch in the 1962 film *To Kill a Mockingbird*, which earned him the Academy Award for Best Actor. He made numerous television appearances and was equally fond of literature.

In June 1971, I worked with him on a special event for the Motion Picture Relief Fund and in May 1975, continuing his support of the film industry, he hosted an evening with Lillian Gish to commemorate the issuance of a D. W. Griffith stamp by the US Post Office. D. W. Griffith was best remembered as the director of *The Birth of A Nation* (1915), which starred the indomitable Miss Gish and was the highest grossing film of the era.

After I had started my own company, Event Management, one of my new clients was the Los Angeles Library Foundation. There was a lot of activity at the Library in downtown LA, and Mr. Peck would participate in any number of evenings where he and other celebrities would read passages from distinguished literary pieces – books, plays, poetry, and so on – and engage in lively discussions with Q&A afterwards.

In 1986, the year director Billy Wilder received AFI's annual accolade, Peck called me personally to request the purchase of a table at the event. It was so nice when celebrities who would have been sent a complimentary invitation anyway made a point of supporting fundraising efforts with their own financial contribution. Needless to say, he was rewarded with one of the best tables in the house!

Jerry Moss, my former boss at A&M Records, was not so fortunate. He had left it rather late when his request for a table came in and we were totally sold out. Of course, I tried to move heaven and earth to get him in and even called Angie Dickinson, who was coming with a group of friends to see if she could squeeze a couple more at her table, but to no avail. In the end we managed to put an extra table virtually on the stage, which sounded great in theory but in practice was dreadful. It was right on the side with virtually zero sight lines to the two huge screens on each side reflecting the show. The sound was bad, and I don't think to this day he has forgiven me. I did my best but seriously wondered if it might have been better to just say no. He never did come again.

In 1989 AFI honored Gregory Peck with its Life Achievement Award, which meant many planning sessions prior to the event. However, most of them were not with the great man himself, but rather his wife Veronique. Of all the tributes over the years, no spouse was ever as involved as Veronique. She was fiercely protective and would come by the office, complete with her little dog, and instruct us as to how everything should be handled. She took the entire process very seriously, and it was obviously of extreme importance to her that the evening was the best it could possibly be. I don't think Mr. Peck had any idea that she had become so involved. They obviously weren't discussing it with each other as he called one day and asked me if anyone was going.

AFI took a very personal interest in the success of each Tribute Dinner, as was shown when I was asked to phone Jimmy Stewart to see if he was planning to attend. Knowing that the Stewarts had just returned from a cruise to Antarctica a few days earlier, George Stevens, Jr. wanted to make sure they had remembered the date. When I called the Stewart residence, Jimmy's wife Gloria picked up the phone. She was so appreciative -- as it turned out they hadn't got it calendared and of course would love to come. At the end of our conversation she told me it was colder here in Los Angeles, this being February 6, 1989, than it had been on the cruise.

Mr. Peck's evening, held on March 9, was star-studded, indeed. I particularly remember thinking what a perfect combination of professional elegance the evening became as Audrey Hepburn hosted the proceedings, introducing fellow actors who paid tribute to Peck's overwhelming body of work over the years. Hepburn had won an Academy Award for *Roman Holiday,* the delightful romantic comedy in which she and Peck had starred during the early part of her career.

The evening was televised on March 21, and it was the first time I got screen credit as the "Dinner Coordinator." Not only that, my name was on the screen all by itself, not in the usual very rapid crawl at the end where you can't possibly read all the names. I nearly fell off my living room sofa as it was totally unexpected. I was thrilled to bits and very impressed with myself!

* * * * *

Chapter Eleven

Natalie Wood blew cigarette smoke in my face as we talked about her role with James Dean in *Rebel Without A Cause* and how she felt she had never really understood him.

Apologizing for the smoke, she continued talking about him as we sat on the floor with our feet under a coffee table in the presidential suite of the Beverly Hilton Hotel, in Beverly Hills, commenting although he had been great to work with, he was very deep. Also, she added they were both very young!

It was Tuesday, March 1, 1977, and the occasion was a party following AFI's tribute to Bette Davis. The room was full of celebrities who had participated in the tribute including Robert Wagner, to whom Natalie Wood was then married for the second time, Gregory Peck, Henry Fonda, Michael Douglas, Mia Farrow, and Jean Marsh, with of course Ms. Davis herself holding court.

RJ, as Robert Wagner liked to be called by his friends, was working with Stefanie Powers on the popular television series *Hart to Hart* at that time, and I was working with Stefanie on some of the William Holden Wildlife Foundation fundraising events. I remember talking to Mr. Wagner that evening and saying what a fan I was of Natalie's. He encouraged me to go and talk to her saying she was just a regular person, like anyone else. It seemed they were the perfect example of "Love is Lovelier, the Second Time Around" since, according to crew members, RJ would make innumerable phone calls from his set to Natalie pretty much on the hour when filming *Hart to Hart*.

The Wagners were very supportive of the arts and would attend various functions to generate interest and attendance. During my years at AFI, I met them on several occasions when their presence helped tremendously. They always looked so beautiful together. I remember wondering how on earth Natalie always managed to get her hair to look so glossy, but never did get the chance to ask her.

In their early days, the Wagners were frequent patrons of La Scala, the restaurant James Dean had helped create with his friend Jean Leon. Dean and Leon had become friends in the 1950s, and both had a dream of opening an upscale meeting place for their show business friends, where they could enjoy gourmet food and fine wines. James Dean pledged a financial investment, and Jean Leon leant his professional business expertise. La Scala finally became a reality in 1956. The opening was a little later than planned due to the untimely death of James Dean in September 1955, after which Jean Leon had to enlist the missing financial support from other friends who shared their fantasy. There is a collage on the wall of Jean Leon's winery outside Barcelona, Spain showing stars like Paul Newman and Joanne Woodard, Groucho Marx, Ava Gardner, Tony Curtis, Jayne Mansfield, John Kennedy, Humphrey Bogart and Lauren Bacall, Denis Hopper, and many others enjoying the restaurant's sumptuous offerings.

I think Natalie Wood epitomized the incredibly difficult life of a major movie personality. Beginning her career at the age of five as a child star, she was one of the few to continue on to adulthood maintaining the same, if not more success. However, she seemed pulled in every direction by family, especially her domineering mother and impossible work schedules, which inevitably would lead to the psychiatrist's couch. I remember Nancy Livingston, who was nominated for her best supporting actress role in *Sunset Boulevard,* saying she was a hostess's nightmare because wonderful as she was it was almost inevitable she would call fifteen minutes before a party to say she couldn't make it.

Chapter Eleven

A life cut short at the age of 43, Natalie Wood left a remarkable legacy behind that will be remembered for a long time, but *I* remember the cigarette smoke best.

* * * * *

One of the most beautiful women in the world – a phrase used to describe Elizabeth Taylor on many occasions – I would initially encounter in the elevator of the Beverly Hilton Hotel in February 1978. George Stevens, Jr., who knew her well, his father having directed one of her most memorable performances in *Giant* in 1956, introduced us. I hadn't realized how petite and even rather fragile she was as she jumped in fright when the doors began to close on her before George put his arm out to prevent that happening. George and I were at the hotel working on that year's Tribute Dinner honoring Henry Fonda, which would take place March 1.

Years later, in 1993, when Miss Taylor was honored with the same award, a much more intimate meeting occurred.

A group of six of us were seated in a private room at the Beverly Hilton Hotel discussing the menu to be served at her Tribute a few weeks later. The occasion was unique in that the honoree rarely attended these gatherings in person. Usually we would have to get input from an associate about their individual likes and dislikes. But this time, together with her dog and her assistant, all of whom occupied independent seats at the table, she was able to add her personal preferences right there and then. Asked her favorite vegetable, she chuckled before announcing it was the modest English pea. She added that the dessert should be chocolate and elaborate but more important, totally decadent. She also added that she would be going on a diet both before and after the event. Married to Larry Fortensky, her seventh husband, she said he, too, needed to go on a diet although raising those beautiful eyes to the sky, she admitted it seemed doubtful.

And yes, in person and close up, she did have those famous dramatic violet blue eyes veiled beneath natural double lashes. I could see them very clearly seated right next to her at that test luncheon.

As promised, she did, indeed, look fabulous on "The Night," and I remember that in her acceptance speech she referred to all the film clips shown during the evening, modestly saying "I wasn't really that bad, was I?"

But she almost didn't get to give an acceptance speech at all!

Cocktails were scheduled to end at 7:30pm, and curtains screening the main ballroom were drawn back, revealing 120 tables shimmering in candlelight awaiting the guests. Armed with seating booklets, everyone wove their way to their respective tables to await the entrance of the honoree. This was always a worrying time for me as I would have to deal with those who were unhappy with their locations or found too many people at one table. That was when the most problem solving went on. I was greatly relieved when the majority were seated, but equally disturbed at the appearance of a white-faced catering manager who pulled me to one side in great agitation. "There's a bomb scare," she said, "and the General Manager is deciding as we speak whether to believe it." Apparently, a phone call had come in stating that a bomb in the underground parking lot (which was right below the ballroom) would detonate at 8pm. By now it was about ten minutes before the hour of doom, and the decision being made as to whether we should evacuate the ballroom.

Linda Kent, the catering manager, and I stood at the back of the ballroom wondering what to do next. It's impossible to describe how I felt at that moment and equally impossible to know how anyone would feel under those circumstances unless one had gone through it. Were we going to die in a matter of minutes? If that were the case, we decided we'd go out in a blaze of glory with champagne in hand so quickly acquired two glasses of Krug feeling at least we'd go out in style!

It would have been impossible to get everyone out in less than ten minutes, and would quite possibly have led to a total panic. In the end, it was decided to treat it as a hoax, which obviously it was, as I'm here to tell the tale, but it was one of the most harrowing moments of my life. Fortunately, none of the guests had a clue what might have happened and the show went on as planned.

*****

As I mentioned earlier, it was during my first week of employment at The American Film Institute I first met Charlton Heston. That same week in November 1974, I had another memorable moment when I walked into my new office at 9am to find Mr. Heston sitting at my desk typing! (This was the 1970s, and we didn't have computers or even word processors yet). "I hope you don't mind my using your typewriter," he said. Well, of course I didn't mind – it would have been somewhat unseemly for me to say I did, so I offered to do the typing for him, but he said he was happy to do it himself. He was on the Board of Trustees, and explained that he would need that document at the meeting, which was taking place later that morning.

The following month, the day after a minor earthquake, I bumped into him again. Having just completed a starring role in the film *Earthquake*, he joked his "earthquake" had been much bigger.

Charlton Heston was very supportive of AFI and participated in many of the social events and fundraising projects during the year in addition to board meetings. He helped make the first film cruise we organized even more memorable by not only hosting a bon voyage cocktail party on board for the special guests sailing that day, but also by donating a men's doubles tennis match on his private court for the auction we would hold at the end of the cruise.

One day I had to deliver some papers to Mr. Heston's estate on Mulholland Drive, an exclusive street stretching for miles high above the city of Los Angeles with impressive homes and fabulous views on all sides. After being let through the gates, I was greeted by four huge German Shepherds bounding up to my little MGB sports car in a very enthusiastic albeit somewhat intimidating manner. Being a dog-lover, I wasn't overly concerned, although I did wait for someone to come from the house and officially organize their welcome before I actually got out of the car. Of course the dogs were soppy, friendly, and gorgeous, but I don't think the Hestons were ever burgled.

Known as a bit of a male chauvinist, he refused to use "Ms." Anybody, and always insisted it be Mrs. or Miss. His secretary Carole would go crazy knowing how much some of us would have preferred being addressed as Ms., but he wasn't having any of it.

In those days, Chuckles (as most of the staff at AFI called him, never knowing whether or not he knew it) drove a Corvette. I remember watching him get in and out with great agility despite the fact that he was a big man, over six feet tall with very broad shoulders – as anyone who has seen *Ben-Hur* will attest.

He appeared in London's West End in a production of *The Caine Mutiny Court Martial* at the Queen's Theatre in 1985 while I happened to be there on vacation, and it was arranged that my friends and I attending the performance would go backstage and say hello after the show. We duly showed up at the stage door only to be told that Mr. Heston's dressing room was a zoo and there was not an inch of space to spare so we were denied entry. Feeling somewhat humiliated and foolish in front of my friends, I don't think I ever totally forgave him, though in retrospect maybe he knew all about "Chuckles" and I got what I deserved.

When I left AFI and formed my own company handling special events for a variety of new clients, he wrote me a lovely note wishing me well. He remains one of the most unforgettable of characters in my life.

* * * * *

In 1971 Loretta Young starred in a film called *Sirens of the Sea*, so it was somewhat ironic that I should meet her at sea aboard "The Love Boat" – the *Pacific Princess*. She lived up to her "siren" image all those years later and was very much the star of the show on The American Film Institute's first movie-themed cruise.

It was Friday, January 6, 1978, when AFI launched its first film cruise from Los Angeles down the Mexican coast to Puerto Vallarta and back to LA, via Mazatlan and Cabo San Lucas. It started with a bang when Charlton Heston hosted his champagne "sail away" on board wishing everyone bon voyage. In those days, security was not something anyone bothered about and visitors were encouraged to celebrate with their departing friends and only requested to disembark some half an hour prior to the ship leaving port.

Loretta Young and her daughter Judy Lewis, who at that time was merely rumored to be Clark Gable's love child – Loretta didn't admit it until 1999 - were joined by Dana Andrews, best remembered for his detective role in Otto Preminger's 1944 film *Laura* and for *The Best Years of Our Lives* with his wife Mary Todd. Renowned lecturer, composer, and film music aficionado Arthur Kleiner rounded out the group with Michael Webb from AFI, who had put the whole film program together and gathered the illustrious guests.

AFI members took over a group of cabins on the ship. The *Pacific Princess* had been chosen because it had a particularly large two-tiered movie theatre accommodating 35mm film. Our stars, together with AFI guests, could watch films on a grand scale, after which there were cocktail gatherings and Q & A sessions to enjoy. We also held an auction of film memorabilia, the items for which I had been responsible for accumulating. Among the acquisitions I had received were a coffee mug from John Wayne, an Italian silk tie from Fred Astaire, and three pots of homemade honey from Henry Fonda, who, unbeknown to most of us, was an avid beekeeper. This last item had a unique caveat attached in that because, due to agricultural restrictions, the honey would not be allowed back into California, the lucky recipient once back in Los Angeles would have to go to Henry Fonda's home in Bel Air and collect it from him personally! All in all, we had 68 items ranging from autographed sheet music framed and signed by Frank Sinatra from his 1954 recording of "All of Me," a (thoroughly now outdated) Betamax Video Recorder, a pipe smoked by Gregory Peck in *MacArthur* (his latest film at the time), an army cap worn by Elvis Presley in 1960's *G.I. Blues,* and a waistcoat Jack Nicholson wore throughout the filming of his just completed picture *Going South.* The whole event turned out to be a great success.

The circumstances surrounding one particular item however became a topic of conversation throughout the ship. I mentioned earlier how movie mogul Irwin Allen had become the master of disaster movies, with perhaps his most famous production being *The Poseidon Adventure.*

Chapter Eleven

The poster advertising the film showed a ship turned upside down due to a tsunami. The surviving passengers had to climb from the top deck (now at the bottom of the sea) to the base of the hull, (now the only level above water). The poster became a collector's item. Mr. Allen had signed one such poster especially for our auction and we left it until last as we sailed along.

Unbelievable as it sounds, (but anyone who was on board will tell you this is absolutely true) the proudly displayed poster taking center stage on an easel in the middle of the room was the item up for sale when the ship hit a rogue wave and listed so violently that all the glasses in the bar smashed to the floor, chairs slid all over the place, and the poster crashed to the ground! Of course the ship righted itself pretty much immediately. Apart from the damage in the bar, all was well and there were no injuries, but it really was a remarkable coincidence. I can't remember if anyone bid on the poster or not!

The day we docked in Puerto Vallarta, Loretta invited us to join her and visit friends who had a fabulous house on a cliff overlooking the sea. The friends weren't there, but the staff was, and we were supplied with a wonderful lunch and towels for the pool. At the foot of the cliff was a natural rock formation rather like a blowhole combined with a Jacuzzi. There were many, many steep steps down the sheer side of the face of the cliff but once at sea level, it flattened out. Waves continuously broke over the rocks before being carried back out to sea, only to be immediately replenished by new ones crashing over us. Extending out into the foaming water was a flat rocky promontory, which although slippery allowed a walk at sea level between the breakers and a few members of our group decided to check it out. Looking back and waving at the rest of us, they didn't see a huge wave coming up behind them until it crashed over them and they were thrown to the ground. Luckily, the receding current didn't take them with it. One guy's glasses were ripped off his face and swept out to sea, and the others had scrapes and bruises on legs and forearms, but fortunately there were no major injuries. None of us remained there much longer, though, preferring to return to the peace and serenity of the pool above. The steps didn't seem nearly so steep on the way back either!

As we returned to the ship, we stopped and did some shopping. Judy and I bought really beautiful Mexican dresses, and Loretta gave us a shawl to go with them. We had a perfectly delightful day. Every time I wear that outfit I remember it well.

The auction brought in close to $9,000, so certainly could be considered a success. I have to admit it never occurred to me as I left the ship I should have acknowledged I was carrying that amount of cash through customs.

* * * * *

Stefanie Powers and I have one very important characteristic in common. We both love animals – quite possibly more than people.

We were first introduced in her trailer in Burbank in November 1982, on the set of *Hart to Hart*, during the show's popular run from 1979 to 1984. Robert Wagner stopped by, which was nice, but the big thrill for me was meeting and having a cuddle with Freeway, the canine star of the series.

We were focusing on fundraising events for the William Holden Wildlife Foundation, however, not the TV show. From 1972, during a nine-year relationship with actor William Holden, Stefanie was introduced to what would become a lifelong passion for the preservation of wildlife. This led to her starting the William Holden Wildlife Foundation in his memory in 1982, a year after his untimely death.

One of the most successful fundraisers I helped her with was at Will Rogers State Park in Pacific Palisades, where a celebrity Polo Match was to take place. An avid horsewoman herself, Stefanie persuaded Robert Wagner, who needed no encouragement and was always very supportive of his *Hart to Hart* co-star, to join in the festivities.

Working on projects for and with Stefanie was great fun as I really believed in the cause, so much so that I didn't charge a fee. In my entire career, she was the only one who ever fell into the gratis category. We had planning sessions in some of the most interesting locales, like dinner one night at the Kingdom of Stallions in Buena Park. We were checking out suitable locations in which to hold a fund-raising Polo Match. A prancing dressage of Andalusian horses would have made a great introduction to our evening, but sadly the organization didn't make enough money to stay in business.

Eventually it was decided to use the Equestrian Center in Burbank, with Patrick Terrail and his Ma Maison eatery of West Hollywood handling the catering. Ma Maison in those days was THE place to be seen dining and it became famous not only for the wonderful food (a young Wolfgang Puck was the chef) and star-studded clientele, but it had an unlisted phone number. It was therefore considered the epitome of chic. Patrick was a master of manipulation in the publicity field, making sure the rich and famous had the number, but kept it a closely guarded secret. I can't remember why or how I had it, but I did.

Occasionally we would meet at Stefanie's house, being greeted on arrival by an array of her pets. She had a parrot, two dogs, and a cat, all of whom were devoted to her, so much so that one of the dogs became extremely adept at finding a way into her car before she left for work, thus making it necessary to go wherever she was going. It became a daily ritual and constant challenge to see who could reach the car first.

On October 23, 1983, about 2,500 people trooped into the Equestrian Center to attend the Polo Match. As well as Robert Wagner and Stefanie herself, other riders included actor William Devane, who began playing Presidential roles in 1974 as John F. Kennedy in *The Missiles of October* and would continue in a similar vein, from *The West Wing* to the recent television series *24*. He just looked like a president, or how we all felt a president should look. The match was a very successful project, raising $125,000. Now, over 35 years later, the William Holden Wildlife Foundation is still flourishing with Stefanie continuing to spend a lot of time in Kenya.

Her newsletter tells of continuing progress in areas not only concerned with conservation, but in the training and education of young students from all over East Africa. Stefanie is also one of the most delightful and lovely people I have ever met.

* * * * *

In 1978, when a second film cruise was planned, I was given the responsibility of organizing it again. This time we were on the *Royal Viking Sea*, and our celebrity guests were Olivia de Havilland, her daughter Gisele, Glenn Ford with his new young bride Cynthia, and veteran director King Vidor with his daughter Belinda.

One of Olivia de Havilland's favorite films was *The Adventures of Robin Hood*, a 1938 film in which she co-starred with major heartthrob and prominent romantic leading man Errol Flynn. Livie, as she asked that we call her, regaled us with stories about the filming and revealed that she had a huge crush on Mr. Flynn, which made the days a lot more interesting. She couldn't wait for him to arrive on the set. But it didn't do her any good; he paid her absolutely no attention at all!

Then there was the time when *Robin Hood* was being shown in some small mid-western town and the theatre owner told her that her name was too long for his marquee and she would have to shorten it. Miss de Havilland responded in no uncertain terms – "Oh no, my dear man, you will just have to extend your marquee!"

Aboard ship, Gisele spent most of the time in a corner of the swimming pool glued to a book, while her mother was constantly losing her spectacles. It became a standing joke, and every time we got up from a table, be it in the dining room, in a lounge, in her cabin, wherever, someone would have to ask if she had her glasses. On one occasion, when we were on a shore excursion and had been to a church to admire the stained glass windows, she wasn't reminded by anyone, and sure enough, we had to return and found them on a pew.

The day the ship docked in St. Maarten, a beautiful island in the Caribbean, we had a bit of an adventure. In a rented car, AFI's Michael Webb was our driver, and we decided to explore the island's coast road, which was supposed to go in a continuous loop so you came back to where you started from. The scenery was gorgeous, and the sea an amazing shade of blue. The only thing that started to deteriorate was the road. We had left just after an early lunch, and with the ship not sailing until 6pm, we felt there was plenty of time for our little jaunt. As the road got worse, our progress got slower. After a couple of hours, we began to wonder whether we would get around the next bend! We kept wondering whether we should turn around and go back, but by then we had gone so far that it seemed it must be shorter to keep going. The road eventually got to the stage where it virtually petered out, and we had no choice but to return from whence we came. This was going to take some time, and the journey became harrowing to say the least. Trying not to keep looking at our watches and pretending there was plenty of time, it got closer and closer to six o'clock. There were no cell phones in those days to let the ship know we were on our way, and we finally reached the pier with literally seconds to spare before they raised the gangway. Later on (after an amazingly quick shower and change), we made our appearance at a pre-arranged cocktail party in the captain's cabin. After he realized who we were and commenting quite amiably, "so you're the group who almost missed the ship," we weren't sure if we should accept his comment as some sort of celebrity status, or be contrite. In the end we just had another glass of champagne and moved on to dinner.

Olivia de Havilland is probably one of the most elegant women you will ever meet. Charming, proper, and polite, you could never imagine her doing anything ungainly or awkward so one afternoon on the beach when she removed her pantyhose to stay cool and go paddling at the water's edge, it was no surprise that she did it with great grace and charm. She did not put them back on, however, nor did she leave them behind with her glasses.

At the conclusion of the cruise, I had meetings at AFI at its East Coast headquarters in Washington, so I flew there with Livie and Giselle while the others returned to Los Angeles. Giselle went on to Paris, but Livie was staying in Alexandria so we dropped her off, making sure she had her spectacles, and I went on to attend the Kennedy Center Honors, the television award show created by George Stevens, Jr. The honorees that year were Marian Anderson, a celebrated African-American contralto and "goodwill ambassadress" for the US State Department,

Fred Astaire, choreographer extraordinaire George Balanchine, composer Richard Rodgers, and the pianist Arthur Rubinstein. What an amazing twenty-four hours that turned out to be!

* * * * *

Another larger than life character, in more ways than one, was Orson Welles.

A truly legendary figure, Orson Welles covered every aspect and every facet in the world of cinema. He was an actor, director, writer, and producer, not to mention his work in theatre and radio. He is probably best remembered for *Citizen Kane,* which he co-produced, directed, and starred in – all at age 25!

In 1943 his portrayal of Mr. Rochester in *Jane Eyre* was particularly impressive and had become one of my roommate's favorite films. She had a crush on Mr. Wells and consequently practically had a heart attack when answering the phone one evening to a voice identifying himself as Orson Welles. It was February 1975, and he was to be honored by AFI that year. He asked for me as there were some script changes he wanted to dictate on the phone. With great reluctance my roommate handed me the phone and I duly noted his requests. I had to pass him on to the producer for further discussion and couldn't engage in a lengthy conversation, but it was another call not to be forgotten.

On February 9, 1975, Welles received his award at a ceremony held at the Century Plaza Hotel in Los Angeles. In addition to phone communications prior to the date of the Tribute, there were also some rather fraught situations caused by his demanding personality and commanding presence. Unused to anyone questioning his behavior, he was a little bit naughty about some of the travel and hotel accommodation arrangements. It was normal practice for AFI to arrange first-class air travel and a luxurious hotel for the honoree. If the honoree didn't live in the United States, round trip tickets would be issued for two, assuming a spouse or significant other would also be attending. Orson Welles allegedly "lost" his air tickets and somehow through the grapevine it was suspected he hadn't lost them at all, but switched them for economy and pocketed the difference. Then to add insult to injury, since he had no intention of traveling in economy, he insisted that the first-class tickets be reissued. Whether or not this was true will never be known, although we definitely had to reissue two more first-class round-trip tickets. The matter was irrelevant anyway because he could hardly have been confronted without great embarrassment, so AFI just bit the bullet and did as he instructed!!!

Welles also refused the accommodations offered at the Century Plaza Hotel, where the dinner was being held, preferring a little boutique hotel called the Carriage House, in Westwood. To say he was a large man at that time would have been an understatement. Hotel staff were heard to say when using their rather intimate elevator, he touched all sides while ascending to his suite.

Welles's special evening remains particularly memorable to me, however, because at that particular occasion I was introduced in person to Frank Sinatra. Needless to say, this did not make the evening special for Mr. Sinatra. He had been the host of the show and was much more interested in receiving accolades from his peers, but to me it was wonderful!

* * * * *

And then there was Jack Nicholson!

What can you say about Jack Nicholson? He is a total law unto himself who can get away with just about anything because he is such a brilliant actor, his talent seems to outweigh any possible transgressions!

Tuesday March 9, 1976, I had my first encounter with the great Mr. Nicholson and I remember it well, although I very much doubt he did. Director William Wyler was being honored by AFI, and Jack was propping up the bar during the opening reception. He looked down at me through those famous hooded bedroom eyes with complete disinterest and I was reminded of the phrase "the lights are on but nobody's home." I respected him as a very fine actor, but the stories about his personal life (although you can't believe everything you read!) left a lot to be desired. I don't doubt he was equally unimpressed with me.

Jack Nicholson's own Life Achievement Award Tribute in 1994 was particularly memorable because of his entrance. Known for wearing Ray Ban sunglasses, we made arrangements to have hundreds of pairs donated for the evening. As the lights dimmed and the announcer intoned, "Ladies and Gentleman, the recipient of the 1994 Life Achievement Award, Mr. Jack Nicholson," as tradition dictated, he entered the ballroom from backstage and made his way through a standing ovation from all 1,200 guests to the head table, shaking hands and greeting everyone with hugs and kisses. Imagine his reaction when he realized everyone had donned a pair of his signature Ray Bans! Never really quite sure what to expect from him, he fortunately found it very funny. Indeed, it was quite a sight to see 1,200 people all wearing the sunglasses in a darkened ballroom. It made for a spectacular opening of the show.

Part of his acceptance speech was anything but amusing, however. Referring to the head table, which was ladies only and included his girlfriend Rebecca Broussard along with Candice Bergen, Cher, Faye Dunaway, Ellen Barkin, Louise Fletcher, Shirley Maclaine, Mary Steenburgen, and Kathleen Turner, he commented how lucky we were that Rebecca had come at all. It seemed she had not wanted to attend, but Jack appreciated the effort and said he would like to thank her for that and, almost as an afterthought, he also thanked her for being the mother of *some* of his children! There was a universal groan from the entire audience, particularly the women in the room, and it was cut from the television broadcast that aired a few weeks later.

At the same time as I was working on Jack Nicholson's event, I was simultaneously handling another fundraising dinner, this time for the Salvation Army. There were innumerable meetings on both sides, and they couldn't have been more different. In the Nicholson office, although he was rarely present, his cohorts continually used the "f" word and constantly referred to their "mothers" along with a lot of other derogatory remarks. Of course, the reverse was the case at the Salvation Army offices. It was decorum at its best, although I was apprehensive about the event's outcome as, maintaining their image, they insisted no alcohol be served, not even wine with dinner. Knowing fundraising events as I did, I knew how hard it was to get people to buy tickets under the most enticing conditions. But to expect them to go to a reception and dinner with not even a glass of wine could well prove to be an impossibility! The powers that be said guests could purchase liquor from a bar inside the LA Convention Center, where the event was to be held, although how they would find it would be another matter. Assuming they did find a bar, I also seriously questioned how they would feel about forking out more money having already paid hundreds of dollars for a ticket to buy a drink! However, I was overruled by the hierarchy.

Lack of alcohol was just one of many differences of opinion. One day, after a very heated meeting with the Nicholson people complete with aforementioned language, I went straight to the Salvation Army headquarters and arrived just in time to begin the meeting there. We were going over the invitation and the timing of everything, and they were dithering over what I considered utterly irrelevant details. In my opinion, the discussion should have been making more of an effort to ensure the evening was a more attractive sell. They were driving me mad. Eventually in a fit of total frustration, I declared "Jesus Christ, what the hell do you think you're doing, you're creating a nightmare and a total disaster!" Although I wasn't fired on the spot and continued to the end of what turned out to be a rather unsuccessful event with very little financial gain, I never worked for the Salvation Army again.

* * * * *

One of the most supportive couples in the Hollywood community was Michael and Pat York. I bumped into them on many occasions as they attended any number of charity events, theatre opening nights, premieres of movies, and so on. They were also great supporters of the Los Angeles Public Library programs.

One of the Library Foundation's most celebrated fund-raising affairs happened every two years and turned into one of the most popular events ever held in Los Angeles. It became unique in that all the guests *enjoyed* the experience, which was not a common outcome for a charity event! It was a standing joke in LA that when invited to a fundraising dinner, you could look forward to a limp salad, prime rib, and ice cream while being thoroughly bored by the head of some probably very worthwhile organization giving an interminable acceptance speech and thanking people you had never heard of. The volunteer ladies who worked on these events had closely guarded guest lists, but it was a vicious circle of purchase, with friends who had been on committees in the past expected to reciprocate as guests when invited by the very friends who had bought tables from them. Inevitably this led to a lot of the same people duplicating attendance. The Library Foundation knew this and one year in what turned out to be a very successful attempt to avoid such a situation, sent an invitation suggesting guests "Stay home and read a book." A lot of people did just that and merely sent a check!! It was a lot less work.

The Literary Odyssey Dinner evenings were different though. Here's how they worked. Invitations would be issued for a series of individual dinner parties all held on the same date in various different locales throughout the city. They would be held in private homes, and a prominent author would be added to host the evening. So Mr. and Mrs. John Smith would give a dinner party in their home with Mr. Charles Dickens as the special guest author to talk about his latest book. It was an intoxicating cocktail of opportunity offering the chance to spend a unique evening with your favorite author in exclusive surroundings with a very small number of additional guests while enjoying a gourmet dinner. This, indeed, proved to be true, although the logistics of putting it all together were challenging to say the least.

The first one was held on Monday, November 17, 1997, and the invitation alone was a monstrous task. It had to contain the name of the host, the name of the author, and the location of the dinner. In addition, it had to detail what the author had written, describe each individual house, state the maximum number of guests who could attend, and announce the dress code. Here are a few examples of the choices in 1997:

Chapter Eleven

Irish "Ayes"

Join co-hosts Pam Mullin and Mayor Richard Riordan for an evening guaranteed to bring out the lad and lassie in everyone. In a beautiful Hacienda-style home, you will be "piped" into dinner by Irish Pipers. After dinner, watch a lively exhibition of Irish step dancing. Joining the party will be **FRANK McCOURT**, Pulitzer Prize winner for the memoir of his Irish childhood, *Angela's Ashes*. And that's no blarney!

50 guests, Mandevillle Canyon, casual attire

Hosts: Pam Mullin and Mayor Richard Riordan

Hail Britannia

Join the British Consul General and his wife in their 1927 California Spanish home, one of designer Wallace Neff's first Los Angeles creations. **JULIA BARRETT (JULIA BRAUN KESSLER)**, whose latest book, *The Third Sister* is a sequel to *Sense and Sensibility* will share her lifelong passion for Jane Austen's extraordinary characters.

12 guests, Hancock Park, cocktail attire

Hosts: The British Consul General and Mrs. Merrick Baker-Bates

(The) Cello, China (and the) Comical

Feast on a Chinese banquet at a traditional 20s Mediterranean home with **MARK SALZMAN,** author of *Iron and Silk* and *The Soloist*. Renaissance man Salzman, a China hand and a cellist, will recall his China experiences with Kung Fu and language and delight with observations of life's absurdities. He'll even play his cello!

12 guests, Brentwood, Chinese attire optional

Hosts: Mickey and Gordon Bodek

People of Substance

In honor of your guest, British-born writer **BARBARA TAYLOR BRADFORD**, a miniature English Garden of her books will sprout from your hosts' dining table. Bradford's bestsellers, such as *A Woman of Substance, Hold the Dream* and *To Be the Best,* are filled with wealth, intrigue and love. Meet her in a villa-like setting, replete with English and French country furniture and eclectic antiques. Unique flavors and food will abound.

15 guests, Holmby Hills, black tie

Hosts: Brindell and Milton Gottlieb, Sue and Irwin Russell & Sheila and Wally Weisman

The hosts went to an inordinate amount of trouble. Barbara Taylor Bradford's hosts planned well in advance and did, indeed, have the dining room table planted to look like a miniature English garden, which took several weeks.

This was not the most difficult part though – the response card became a logistical nightmare. On the RSVP page, there was space to list the six dinners of your choice in order of preference. But it didn't stop there. The minimum ticket price was $350 per person, for which you were guaranteed one of your six choices. If you felt inclined to splurge, you could pay $1,000 per person and were then guaranteed one of just two dinner choices, not six. Finally, if you had just one author and a selection you couldn't live without, a contribution of $5,000 per couple entitled you to go not only to the evening of your choice, but also to another party the night before the big event where all the hosts and authors would be in attendance.

This was all fine and well until it came time to work out the responses and assign specific dinners to each of the guests. As each dinner had a different number of attendees (depending on the size of the various dining rooms) and some were more popular than others, there was extensive juggling of places and moves from one to another. As time went on, it got more and more complicated.

We also had special arrangements for promotional flights from airlines so that some authors coming in from far away did not have to absorb such an expense. It was the same with the major hotels throughout the city. Most were very accommodating and gave us complimentary rooms knowing this was a fundraising endeavor.

The evening in question was an unqualified success, leading to a continuing trend although from a financial standpoint the end didn't really justify the means. The majority of tickets were sold for $350, so the income wasn't massive. However, as far as good will for the Library, it was priceless.

Michael and Pat York participated frequently in the Literary Odyssey Dinners, both as hosts and guests, with Pat as a writer and Michael an actor, allowing them to fall into both categories. They also frequently attended AFI's Life Achievement Award Dinner, though sometimes if I hadn't heard from them as the date drew close, I would have to call and remind them. Having invariably lost the invitation in the myriad of others received every day, they were always most grateful and appreciative.

* * * * *

Robert Stack had a highly successful career in film and television. Although he starred in over forty feature films, it was his television series, *The Untouchables*, that really made him a household name.

He seemed to have a highly successful and happy marriage to wife Rosemarie as well. They were one of the most beautiful and longest lasting couples in Hollywood, remaining married from 1956 until his death in 2003. Rosemarie loved telling the story of when they met and how she "hooked" him way back when. Apparently, admiring him from afar the first time she saw him, she checked out his daily schedule at the studio and always happened to be around when he finished work or had a break. She was very unassuming and casual but always there, so that one day when she wasn't, he started looking for her. Needless to say, she let herself be found, after which they began dating and the rest as they say is history.

The Stacks were involved in a project I had helped organize in August 1978. The American Film Institute was hosting a UNESCO Symposium in Los Angeles, offering a week's activities to a group of foreign directors. They would experience first-hand the lives of their American counterparts and share their experiences and stories from the other side of the world.

At the initial cocktail party for about 250 invited guests at Greystone Mansion, the socializing began. D'Arcy Hayman, the International Arts Program director for UNESCO, was among the honored guests who participated in the proceedings. Among the other star participants was Geraldine Chaplin, daughter of Charlie.

One of the most successful evenings was held at the Stacks' home in Bel Air. The visiting directors if memory serves, included Costa-Gavras, whose 1969 film *Z* was one of the few films to be nominated for an Oscar in the Best Picture *and* Best Foreign Language categories. Milos Foreman, an Academy award winning director, was there and he would go on to win his second directing Oscar for *Amadeus* in 1984. Fred Zinneman another two-time Oscar winner, also put in an appearance.

It was fascinating to watch the likes of Franklin J. Schaffner, director of *Patton* and always a staunch supporter of AFI, chatting with Stanley Kubrick, director of the infamous *A Clockwork Orange*, while Jan Kadar, who taught a class at AFI and who directed *Lies My Father Told Me* in 1976 conversed with Billy Friedkin of 1971's *The French Connection* fame and who also taught a class at AFI at one point. Franco Zeffirelli, best known for his 1968 version of *Romeo ard Juliet* and his opera productions, could be seen talking to Rouben Mamoulian who had directed one of the first "talkies" in 1929, a film called *Applause.*

On another occasion during this remarkable week, renowned director Arthur Hiller, perhaps best known for directing *Love Story*, invited all the visitors to his home in Bel Air. This was another grand occasion in the most elegant and exotic surroundings. I remember thinking everyone would probably imagine that all successful American film directors lived like this, and in retrospect most of them did.

These evenings were overflowing with creative talent. One of the things that impressed me the most was how thrilled each individual director was to meet another. I realized for the first time that no matter how prominent you are in your own field, it is always a delight to meet your peers and without social occasions such as this, it would probably never happen as graciously.

Chapter Twelve:
Brief Encounters

One of the most dramatic brief encounters occurred in 1982 with Claudette Colbert and Douglas Fairbanks, Jr.

From time to time, if the facilities were available I would set up an office wherever the current event was taking place. Logistically, this made sense as inevitably getting closer to the date it would be necessary to be "on site" for various meetings and discussions. This was the case at the Beverly Hilton Hotel in 1982, when it was director Frank Capra's turn to be honored by AFI. Of course, he had directed the classic *It Happened One Night* starring Claudette Colbert and Clark Gable.

I had set up an office in the hotel's Fountain Room, which had walls of glass looking out directly onto the driveway and the main entrance – due to re-modeling it doesn't exist any more – when all of a sudden, I saw two elderly people emerge from the lobby, look left and right in some confusion, and then head toward our location at some speed. Close on their heels came a group of press photographers together with marauding fans, all eager for pictures and autographs. The couple turned out to be Douglas Fairbanks, Jr. and Claudette Colbert trying to leave via the valet parking after rehearsing for the show. Seeing this somewhat daunting situation unfolding, I jumped up and opened the door to the Fountain Room, which they gladly ran through and then I closed and locked it behind them. After drawing the curtains across the walls of glass our "guests" could relax and recover.

According to Miss Colbert, who was almost 80 at the time and looked absolutely stunning, she hadn't run that fast in quite some time. They were surprised by all the attention, as public appearances were not as frequent as they used to be. They told us the ballroom looked lovely and that the show was going very well based on the other rehearsals they had seen. Of course, memories of *It Happened One Night,* dating back to 1946, were making Claudette feel very nostalgic.

They were most grateful for our hospitality, and we had a lovely time with both until it was safe for them to return outside and retrieve their cars to go home.

* * * * *

On a typically beautiful sunny day in Southern California with the sky an incredible blue and not a cloud in sight, I was to encounter another equally beautiful sight.

It was Wednesday, March 12, 1975, on the occasion of the funeral of George Stevens, the prolific director of films like *Giant* and *A Place in the Sun.* He was also the father of George Stevens, Jr., head of The American Film Institute. I had been given the task of receiving guests as they arrived for a reception following the ceremony – someone other than the caterers needed to be at the house to let them in. Martin Manulis, then Director of the West Coast operation, had offered his home in Bel Air.

So there I was at my post in the living room, making sure the catering firm was on track and that a buffet and bar was in place with half an hour to spare before anyone was expected to arrive. Imagine my surprise then to hear the doorbell ring much sooner than expected, and even more surprised after I opened it.

Chapter Twelve

Framed against the brilliant blue sky stood the epitome of tall, dark, and handsome – the magnificent Rock Hudson! Standing in the doorway, he was accompanied by English actor and professional photographer Roddy McDowell. He apologized profusely for coming early, explaining that they had been pallbearers at Forest Lawn Memorial Park. Once their task had been completed, they decided to leave early so they could relax for a few minutes before anyone else arrived.

"Please come in," I managed to utter, somewhat flustered and trying very hard not to show it as I led the way back into the living room where two couches faced each other flanking the fireplace. We each sat on opposite sides, and I remember thinking at the time this is something I must remember. It's not every day, in fact it's unlikely to be *any* day, that you find yourself seated opposite someone like Rock Hudson.

We had a lovely conversation. Roddy didn't say much, but Mr. Hudson was utterly charming and we talked about remodeling our kitchens and the shenanigans of our dogs – we both had German Shepherds. As George Stevens had directed Rock Hudson in the epic *Giant,* the conversation inevitably changed to movies, both his and others, so time flew by and it seemed no time at all before the bell rang again. After that so many guests wafted in and out, I didn't say much more than "please come in" but never forgot my unique twenty minutes with a superstar. And he was so nice!

* * * * *

During the 1980s, the English actor Anthony Andrews became a big name in the States due to his starring role in the British television series *Brideshead Revisited,* starring Jeremy Irons, which aired on PBS and was a hugely successful series in both countries. I was among the viewers eagerly awaiting the next installment.

A couple of days before AFI's Tribute to Jack Lemmon in 1988, I got a call from the William Morris Agency saying that Anthony Andrews was in town and would like to attend. By then the event was completely sold out, but as I was informed that Mr. Andrews would be coming alone and was a terrific fan of Mr. Lemmon, couldn't I possibly squeeze him in somewhere? Having already decided I would find space, I said I would have to check and see what I could do and get back to them. A suitable time later, I duly called back and said I had worked a miracle and they should send a messenger to pick up the ticket.

The night of the event when I saw Anthony Andrews come in (I had been watching the door very carefully all evening), alone as promised, I felt it my duty to go and say hello and let him know I was responsible for his getting a ticket. I also felt I should let him know that after the dinner and show there was a special after party, to which the celebrities, VIPs, AFI board members, and associates of the honoree were invited. The location was a closely guarded secret, so I explained that I would find him at the conclusion of the show and escort him there myself. I did just that and the two of us proceeded down a passage at the back of the ballroom, into the kitchen, and then through another discreet entrance to the location of the party. This worked very well, and he was thoroughly charming and most appreciative. Two days later a dozen red roses were delivered to my desk with a lovely thank you note, which remains in a very special scrapbook to this day. Interesting to note that on the card accompanying the flowers and mentioning the Tribute, he spelled Mr. Lemmon's name with only one "m!"

* * * * *

Living in the center of the entertainment world, it was inevitable that some surprise encounters would occur. An evening at the Ice House in Pasadena in April of 1982 provided just that when I met Joseph Wambaugh. A former Detective Sergeant in the Los Angeles Police Department, he was famous for his bestselling novels based on his experiences. Probably *The Onion Field* was the best known, but he had a string of top sellers including *The Blue Knight, The Choirboys*, and *The Black Marble*.

Mr. Wambaugh was in the audience on the opening night to see his friend, British singer-songwriter Ian Whitcomb's US debut. Ian was part of the so-called British Invasion, but unlike his counterparts of that era, didn't make the big time.

* * * * *

Another charming and unforgettable character was James Stewart.

Jimmy Stewart, as he was frequently known, was a true Hollywood legend for many, many years. Few other actors played such diverse roles as he - classic Westerns like *The Man Who Shot Liberty Valance* and *Shenandoah,* dramas *Rear Window, The Man Who Knew Too Much,* and *Vertigo,* comedies like *The Philadelphia Story,* classics like *Mr. Smith Goes to Washington,* and perhaps the most timeless of all, *It's a Wonderful Life,* combined to create a real superstar.

The first time I saw him was on the London stage in a production of *Harvey* in August 1975 with English actress Mona Washbourne. It's a classic story about a man who claims to have a best friend named Harvey, whom he describes as a six-foot tall rabbit, but whom nobody else can see. It's a very funny play, which Mr. Stewart had made his own, appearing in the original production on Broadway in the late 1940s, at London's Prince of Wales Theatre in 1949 and at Paris's Théâtre Antoine in 1950. After another Broadway revival in 1970, where Helen

Hayes co-starred with him, it was finally in 1975 that I saw his performance and by then I'm sure he well and truly knew his lines.

In 1980, when he received AFI's Life Achievement Award, a who's who of Hollywood's elite were in attendance to pay their respects. Actors, producers, directors, writers, studio heads, political pundits, publicists, and fans became an enthusiastic audience as the *crème de la crème* of film and television told stories of their encounters and experiences with the great man.

The head table with Mr. and Mrs. Stewart was star studded to say the least. Frank Capra, probably his favorite director, sat with Cary Grant, Henry Fonda, and Grace Kelly, who was by then H.S.H Princess Grace of Monaco. Producer and director hierarchy were also there in force, with Albert (Cubby) Broccoli, associated with almost all the James Bond classics, disaster maestro Irwin Allen, Academy Award-winning director William Wyler, veteran producer Walter Mirisch, and, then becoming a household name for producing television sitcoms like *All in the Family, Sanford and Son, The Jeffersons*, and *Maude,* Norman Lear.

As a tribute to the name of the honoree and to personalize his evening, a square of Stewart tartan fabric had been pasted on the inside cover of the program book given to all the guests. This was the brainchild of that year's Dinner Chairwoman, Mrs. Dennis (Terry) Stanfill, who came up with the idea thinking it would be a nice gesture and probably fairly simple to accomplish. This was not the case, however, as to begin with it proved very difficult to locate the specific Scottish clan associated with the Stewarts and even after finding it, locating fabric we could purchase took countless hours of research. If the internet had been available at that time, we could have googled "Stewart clan tartan" and probably found sources in a trice. Of course, we found it in the end and eventually had several yards sent from London. It did, indeed, add a touch of extra thoughtfulness to the evening. Terry was one of the few chairwomen volunteers who really worked on an event

Not only was James Stewart famous for his acting prowess, he was also known for his charm and gentlemanly manner at all times. He was also a keen gardener, at one time buying the lot next to his home in Beverly Hills to give him more space to play in the dirt.

* * * * *

Although regrettably brief, my encounters with Ernest Borgnine were numerous.

A legendary figure in Hollywood, Ernie (as he liked to be called although his screen credits were always Ernest) Borgnine won an Oscar for his performance as *Marty* in Paddy Chayefsky's 1955 movie. His career changed course after that, and he became a leading man instead of character actor for the next six decades. His fifth wife, Tova, had a line of beauty products, and if her own complexion was anything to go by, they were excellent.

Every year (hence the innumerable albeit brief encounters), the Borgnines would be invited by Sheila and Irwin Allen to attend AFI's event and be seated with countless celebrities who became frequent attendees, including Michael and Shakira Caine, George Burns and a guest (usually a beautiful young starlet and a different one every year!), Mr. and Mrs. Red Buttons, Steve Allen and Jayne Meadows, and Mr. and Mrs. Karl Malden.

By his own admission, Ernie wasn't the best looking of men, but his personality made up for it He had a great capacity for enjoyment at all times, he was beloved by his fellow actors and thoroughly appreciative of his own life and success and more than willing to stay that way.

George Burns was almost always among the guests at the Allen table, but he also attended many, many other social events throughout the year all over Los Angles and could have been the one person to fulfill a dream I always had.

Living in Hollywood and working in film, of course, I loved the Academy Awards every year. One of my ambitions was to go to the Oscars, but there was a caveat – I had to be the guest of a winner! Needless to say, that could very well be why I never achieved this particular ambition, although I think in 1976 the year George Burns was nominated for Best Supporting Actor in *The Sunshine Boys,* if I could have gone with him I would have pulled it off. He was a shoe-in that year and indeed did win.

George was one of those people you can't imagine ever being any different – on camera or off, on the set or at home, it made no difference, he was *always* very funny.

What a wonderful life he had, celebrating his 100th birthday in 1996. His acceptance speech when collecting his Oscar was typically George when he explained, "*I hadn't made a movie for 37 years, but The Sunshine Boys was such fun, I've decided to make another every 37 years from now on.*" He was 80 then!

* * * * *

Around Award season, during the spring each year, more celebrities than usual would be in town to attend the various shows, including the Oscars. After AFI's tribute to Bette Davis in 1977, I was out to dinner in Hollywood at Au Petit Café on Vine Street when I bumped into Geraldine Fitzgerald. A talented actress in many areas including theatre, film, and television, her most significant successes had come with a role in *Dark Victory*, starring Bette, and then as Isabella Linton in William Wyler's *Wuthering Heights* (the 1939 version starring an intense Laurence Olivier), for which she garnered an Academy Award nomination for her supporting performance. By 1976, however, she had begun a new career as a cabaret singer and was about to open with her own show at a club called Studio One in Los Angeles. After our unexpected meeting, she invited my group of friends to be her guests so we were lucky enough to see a great show. She had wonderful presence if not the most stunning voice in the world, and she had a star-studded audience. I met Hermione Baddeley that evening, the English character actress whose name in the UK was mostly associated with one of her most famous films, *The Belles of St. Trinians*, and in the US for television appearances in *Little House on the Prairie* and *Maude*.

* * * * *

I have always been a great fan of what I call fairly heavy-going theatre! I like Ibsen, Chekhov, and Shakespeare, but almost better than anyone I admire Harold Pinter. That is not to say I necessarily understand the dialogue, in fact most of the time I have no idea what's going on and fail to follow the plot, but he has such a way with words that I am always completely absorbed.

One of my favorite plays by Mr. Pinter is *No Man's Land*, which I saw in London in August 1975 with Sir Ralph Richardson and Sir John Gielgud. I was in good company, as Sir Alec Guinness and Margaret Leighton were also in the audience. Sitting in the darkened theatre reveling in the spoken word, I was completely captivated by what was happening on stage although just as I thought I was beginning to understand what was going on, Pinter would throw a curve into the mix and I would be thoroughly confused again. I didn't realize at the time it was the intent of the author to make his audience work hard and really think about what they were watching. I remember thinking how great it would be to have someone with me to compare notes.

At that time, I was working with Martin Manulis, Director of West Coast operations for AFI and a good friend of Sir Ralph. Martin had seen the play earlier in the year and suggested that I congratulate his friend on his behalf.

So here was the perfect opportunity, I thought. After the performance I will go back stage and ask what it's all about – get it straight from the horse's mouth as it were! I duly went to congratulate Sir Ralph on his wonderful performance and asked him if he could explain what was going on, based on my obviously limited comprehension capabilities. With a wonderful bland smile, he turned in his chair towards me and admitted he didn't have a clue, but agreed it was an extraordinary and quite, quite wonderful play! I must say I felt much better.

* * * * *

George Clooney can't help it, he's just plain gorgeous! I met him, albeit much too briefly, at a 1980s fundraising event for the Weingart Center at Universal Studios when he was a working actor on the brink of fame and fortune. The Weingart Center is a wonderful organization helping men and women get off the streets and break the cycle of homelessness and poverty. Being a non-profit group, fundraising events helped swell their coffers, especially when celebrities like George were willing to help.

Later on, after his role in the nighttime soap *Sisters,* which ran in the early 1990s, his star began to climb. But at that time he hadn't

Chapter Twelve

reached the pinnacle of success from which he surveys us all now. Back then, I remember him as charming, friendly, and totally accessible, with a knack for making you think he was just an ordinary guy conversing about the weather. His reputation hasn't changed over the years, and he just keeps getting better looking every time I see him.

* * * * *

Barbara Stanwyck and I shared the same doctor, a fact I discovered the night of her AFI Tribute in April 1987. At the time she was suffering with chronic back pain, and I was told later she had a steel splint in her spine that would at least allow her to walk on stage that night. It was touch-and-go, though, so her physician, Dr. Robert Kositcheck, unbeknown to me at the time, was stationed at her side pretty much all evening.

It was an eclectic mix of celebrities that night, with comedians Chevy Chase and Jim Belushi at tables next to Ann-Margaret, Walter Matthau and Robert Wagner, along with John Travolta, Henry Winkler, and Charlton Heston, as well as Dr. Robert Kositcheck!

In addition to Miss Stanwyck, Dr. K had various other celebrities as patients, including Marlon Brando, another fact I discovered during a hospital stay when I got a late evening visit from him about 11pm – from Dr. K, not Marlon Brando. He appeared wearing a tuxedo and looked very distinguished, having just come from a tribute dinner to Mr. Brando. I remember apologizing to him if he had had to leave early to stop by and see me, but he assured me he would have left then anyway as the following was a workday.

* * * * *

At the conclusion of AFI's Life Achievement Award Tributes, there was an after party in a separate and unknown location just for a select group of celebrities and VIP guests. It was considered a coup to get an invitation, and the location was kept secret (except to those invited) to avoid all 1,200 guests who had attended the earlier part of the evening from crashing. It was also a boon to those selected, providing a more interesting alternative to the long line at the valet parking while awaiting their cars.

A typically star-studded evening took place in 1991, when Kirk Douglas received the award. The "after party" looked like a who's who of Hollywood. Lauren Bacall, Tom Cruise, Karl Malden, Patricia Neal, Angie Dickinson, Jean Simmons, Sylvester Stallone, Dana Carvey, Danny DeVito and wife Rhea Perlman, David Lynch of *Twin Peaks* fame, and Kevin and Cindy Costner mixed and mingled while congratulating Mr. Douglas on his amazing body of work. Kevin had completed *Field of Dreams* and *Dances With Wolves* by then. The following year one of my favorites, *The Bodyguard*, would be released.

I didn't have a lengthy conversation with the Costners that evening because they were too interested in each other to want to bother with anyone else. I remember thinking how wonderful it must be to be that much in love and whether it would ever happen to me. It didn't seem possible that the marriage would break up, though years later, after it had I met Cindy again when she was on a committee involved with a fundraising drive for the Truman Presidential Library and Museum. That wasn't a very successful event and was fraught with delays and mismanagement, but Cindy was a delight.

* * * * *

Dame Judi Dench is probably one of England's greatest assets – and certainly among the most talented. Her whole life spent in the spotlight, she had made classic films, done drama and comedy in the theatre, starred in several British television sitcoms, and can sing, too!

One of her most famous roles was that of "M" in the James Bond films, but I suspect other performances take precedence on her list of favorites. Perhaps *Tea with Mussolini* or *The Best Exotic Marigold Hotel* might stand out, or *Shakespeare in Love*, in which she played Queen Elizabeth I. *Pride and Prejudice* and *Philomena* might also make the grade. I don't think she ever gave a bad performance in her life.

Belonging to BAFTA (British Academy of Film and Television Arts) in Los Angeles, I have often joined other members for preview screenings where frequently the stars, director, or writer were also in attendance participating in Q&A sessions afterwards. It's a great way to form your own opinion of something before being swayed by critical acclaim - or not!

I remember a screening in 2006 of *Notes on a Scandal,* which was a very downbeat film. Dame Judi's part was unsympathetic to say the least, calling for her to look particularly unattractive most of the time!

Being best known in the US for her English comedy television series *As Time Goes By*, reruns of which at that time were shown weekly on PBS, it was a stark contrast to watch her performance and then listen to her answer questions on both dramatic and comedic roles.

As anyone who has seen *As Time Goes By* knows, Judi's character has a particularly irritating sister-in-law who has a nasty habit of saying "Poor Jean" in a very condescending manner under a variety of circumstances. On the night in question I was sitting at the end of a row of seats just above the entrance and could observe the comings and goings of the audience and in this case the stars of the film.

As Judi was making her exit after a fascinating Q&A, the friend I had brought as my guest made the comment, "Poor Jean," which elicited the classic Judi Dench giggle for which she is so famous.

Her version of "Send in The Clowns" from the musical *A Little Night Music* is quite possibly the best of anyone's (even Frank Sinatra). Makes you wonder if there is anything she does not do to utter perfection.

* * * * *

I never heard any kind of negative comment made when talking about Audrey Hepburn. One of the most elegant women in the world, she was gracious and beautiful, both inside and out.

I had a couple of telephone conversations with her when she came to Los Angeles to take part in Fred Astaire's Tribute. As she said in her piece on the show, when she first met Fred on the set of *Funny Face*, she felt both her feet turn to "solid lead." But she overcame that and, if not the most skillful of Fred's dancing partners, she was certainly one of the most graceful.

* * * * *

I have never been formally introduced to Christopher Plummer, but on one occasion in February of 1998, a few days before AFI's Tribute to Robert Wise, he left a message on my answering machine. I played it over and over again, listening intently to his beautiful speaking voice, and felt as if he were my new best friend.

While working on these annual fundraisers for AFI, I would often be in touch with the various celebrities invited to participate in the evening's festivities due to their involvement with each individual recipient. Having played the role of Captain von Trapp in *The Sound of Music,* Plummer had to be there and flew from Canada for the big night.

It was a star-studded evening, hosted by Julie Andrews who introduced all the actors who had played the von Trapp family, all by then thirty years older.

* * * * *

Encounters with some of the biggest names in show business have been so brief as to cause regret that I didn't have more opportunity for conversation. So it was on the evening of Wednesday, March 1, 1978 I met Richard Burton. It was a gathering of special guests at the after party following the Tribute to Henry Fonda. Although I spoke to Mr. Burton, as well as to Mr. Fonda himself, those occasions didn't allow for lengthy chats. That probably was a major relief for the celebrities, but not for me!. That same evening I spoke to James Garner, then at the height of his career having starred in *The Rockford Files*, and Jane Alexander, who years later would go on to chair the National Endowment for the Arts.

* * * * *

There were other brief encounters at which I was not present, but I have it on the best authority these stories are all true!

If you were an usher at CBS Studios on Fairfax Avenue in Los Angeles in the 1970's one of your duties was to escort groups of visitors on tours of the facility. Two stories high, the administration offices were on the first floor and the studios on the second. There was a notoriously slow elevator between the two, and sometimes it would take as long as 5 minutes to ascend. This necessitated small talk to keep the guests occupied. One day, while waiting what seemed an interminable amount of time, one of the ushers told the tale of when on that very spot some years earlier, Mae West had been waiting for that same elevator. She was doing a special for CBS and headed for the studios on Level 2. When the elevator doors finally opened, who should emerge but evangelist Billy

Graham. In a voice deep with Christian concern, the Reverend said, "Ms. West, I prayed for you last night." Ms. West smiled patiently and replied, "Silly boy. Should have phoned."

* * * * *

As a canyon in the Hollywood Hills weaves its way up from Franklin Avenue into Griffith Park, one enters a local market. It used to be named the Mayfair, but then Gelsens put their sign above the door. A frequent shopper there in the 1990s was a slightly scruffy and pretty much unrecognizable Brad Pitt. To this day he still maintains an impressive compound in the neighborhood where he and Angelina Jolie used to enjoy some time off particularly during Academy Award season, as invariably one or both would be up for a trophy!

Long before the days of Angelina, or Jennifer Aniston for that matter, Brad had a wonderful California bungalow, which happened to be adjacent to friends of mine. On one memorable occasion, when my friends were away for the weekend, the lady house-sitting their cat inadvertently set off the alarm on their security system. Despite having the code, she had entered through the back door and dutifully punched in the given numbers to an already beeping panel, but must have done something wrong as all hell broke loose with bells and whistles screaming every which way. Of course, the security company called, saying they had evidence of a break-in. Somewhat panic stricken, the poor girl explained that she was house sitting and must have punched in the wrong numbers, thereby setting off the alarm.

The drama continued with major hammering on the back door to add to the confusion. In desperation and with the phone in one hand, she opened it to find a shirtless Brad Pitt standing there, asking if everything was OK. He had been working in his garden and when he heard the alarm go off, jumped over the fence to see what was going on. Finding that all was well, he returned home, having not only played the Good Samaritan, but providing this young woman with an unforgettable Hollywood experience.

* * * * *

Towards the end of her career, Bette Davis moved into the Colonial House on Sunset Boulevard in the heart of Hollywood. Her immediate neighbors across the hall, a gay couple – in a goodwill welcoming gesture – gifted her a basket of goodies and invited her to their apartment for a drink later in the week. She accepted their invitation and after two cocktails and reasonably genial conversation, took her leave saying what a pleasure it had been and she would reciprocate the following week. An invitation for cocktails duly appeared under their door, which was accepted. Taking their cue from her, after a second drink they took their leave, saying what a pleasure it had been. Bette's parting shot as they made their exit was *"And isn't it nice we won't ever have to do this again."* And they never did!

Chapter Thirteen:
'The Times They Are A-Changin'

"The Times They Are A-Changin," was one of Bob Dylan's most influential songs, which he wrote in 1964. I think each generation feels there has been more change for them than at any other time, and that's quite possibly true for each of those generations except some seem greater than others! The invention of the wheel changed the world the same way Steve Jobs altered world communication with the iPhone.

I think we all remember where we were when the most traumatic events in our lives occurred, leading to inevitable changes.

In the early part of 1992, I was to experience one of the most bizarre and rather terrifying events of my life.

Wednesday, April 29, started the same as any other day. I spent most of it in Beverly Hills at the home of Nancy Livingston (where she had her Oscar nomination certificate for *Sunset Boulevard* hanging in the guest bathroom), who was chairing the opening night of Center Theatre Group's production scheduled for the following Friday and for which we had done a mass mailing of invitations several weeks before. Without the modern technology of today's world, the fastest way to get thousands of invitations sent was to get together a large volunteer committee to hand address the envelopes, collate the sometimes as many as five components (actual invitation, response card, return envelope, permit from the city and list of Honorary Committee members and so on) to go into the envelope. It had to be stuffed in the right order and then the envelope filed alphabetically (so that duplications could be eliminated). A stamp would have to be affixed and taken to the post office. Sometimes after alphabetizing, we were required to resort by ZIP code before delivering. No mean feat, this whole procedure could take as long as a week, with at least six or seven volunteers working all day in a large space that would accommodate such an endeavor.

So there we were seated at Nancy's dining room table going over final details when the verdict in the Rodney King police beating case was announced.

The trial stemmed from a group of LAPD officers who had been videotaped from the balcony of a neighbor's home showing them striking African-American motorist Rodney King after a high-speed car chase in downtown Los Angeles. Part of the footage was aired around the world, where racial tensions were high, and several officers were charged with assault with a deadly weapon and use of excessive force. The jury acquitted the cops.

All hell broke loose immediately. Fires were started all over the city, there were riots and more beatings, murders, and most of South Central LA was in chaos. But it didn't stop there. The fires spread, and by evening the fire departments couldn't keep up. I was staying with people on the West Side so was able to get there from Beverly Hills, but going east back to Hollywood would have been impossible.

The next day, I had a meeting at the Beverly Hilton Hotel regarding AFI's Sydney Poitier Tribute. I got there, but later, as the riots continued to spread, there was nowhere to go. I was stuck. The traffic along Sunset Boulevard was virtually at a standstill, the rioting and looting now in Beverly Hills, along Wilshire Boulevard. Everything in the downtown area was closed. All the shops, supermarkets, gas stations, even the airport – nothing was safe. We had a television monitor put into the office at the Hilton so we could see what was happening. It was totally unbelievable. The staff who had made it to the hotel to work couldn't go home, and the shift due in for the evening weren't able to get there. A curfew was issued from dusk to dawn as the city literally burned itself out.

I really couldn't have chosen a better place to be, as the hotel was pretty much invincible with its own security and massive staff, and also of course plenty of rooms to accommodate those of us who had to stay. As those on duty couldn't get home and those due to take over couldn't get to the hotel, that first evening at dinner I was waited on by the executive staff I was working with. Talk about a reversal of roles – I felt I should offer to do the dishes!

Of course, the big opening night at the Music Center downtown planned for Friday was cancelled. I spent the entire evening on the phone calling as many people as I could to let them know it was all off. Most had already figured that out and couldn't have got to the theatre if they had wanted to anyway, but it was a nice gesture.

The National Guard was called in to quell the disturbances, and the fire department began to get a handle on the situation, which by this time had spread as far south as Long Beach. As I drove out of the city three days later heading south on the freeway, I could still see flames burning in the cold light of day. The curfew in Los Angeles continued through Saturday, and I was very happy to be "out in the sticks" and away from it all.

The postponed Joffrey Gala finally took place on Thursday, May 28, at what had been the Coconut Grove Night Club in the old Ambassador Hotel on Wilshire Boulevard. In its heyday, the Grove had been an upscale establishment with great entertainers gracing its stage. I had seen performers like Eddie Fisher, Nat King Cole, Vikki Carr, and Shirley Bassey there, but the whole venue was more sadly remembered for the assassination of Robert Kennedy in 1968. It was just as well that our party was in the evening. It was dark, and the whole place was dank and depressing despite our attempts to liven it up with decorations and balloons covering the worst cracks and blemishes. The approach to the 3400 block of Wilshire looked like a warzone as a result of the riots, and several burned out buildings not yet repaired were a grim reminder of the violence. It looked like a scene from *Les Misérables* but there wasn't any music!

* * * * *

The assassination of President John F. Kennedy in November 1963 so many years earlier was another of the most significant events in my life. It took place while I was in Spain. Those were crazy and fun days in the early 1960s, before I moved to the States. It seemed I could do anything. With my itchy feet I wasn't content to remain in an office in London so ran away on two occasions to spend the summers at resorts on the south coast of England. Of course, I didn't really run away. Everyone knew where I was. But it felt sort of rebellious to go off and do something different.

The first occasion saw me as a waitress at Butlins holiday camp in Cliftonville near Margate, in the county of Kent, and the second as secretary to the general manager at Pontins Little Canada Holiday Camp on the Isle of Wight, England's lovely island off the south coast of Hampshire.

It was during my sojourn on the Isle of Wight I enjoyed my first real romance, which was what inevitably led to my running away to the

US after it all went wrong and just prior to that the trip to Spain. He was a Bluecoat (they were Redcoats at Butlins) and a singer and entertainer who, I thought, was fabulous. However, it was also during those months I was to meet a new friend whom I would know my entire life and share various historic moments with.

Her name was Audrey Bond (no relation to James), and she worked as the receptionist welcoming guests and taking care of their needs at the front desk when they checked in. We immediately became friends and would frequently go out in the evenings together to all the local pubs and hot spots. The guests never seemed to be very interesting, and we had much more fun socializing with the locals or the other members of the staff, especially my favorite Bluecoat.

It was during this time we decided to save our money, which wasn't difficult as we were living rent free – we shared a sweet little two-bedroom cottage on the grounds called Trappers, had all our meals provided, and only got one day off a week in which to spend our paychecks. A villa in Spain to avoid the dreaded English winter sounded wonderful.

During our time in Spain we heard for the first time a wonderful song from Argentina entitled "Cuando Calienta el sol," and I immediately realized it would become a worldwide hit. Having worked at the New Musical Express newspaper in London and been initiated into the arena of pop music from my preteen years, I felt I was an expert on such matters. I was proved right, of course, and to this day regret I couldn't have jumped on that band wagon and done something with it in the US. But I wasn't even there yet, so I just enjoyed the song.

On Friday, November 22, 1963, Audrey and I were ensconced in the villa on the Island of Majorca and learned of the assassination of

President Kennedy over the radio in Spanish. Being in a foreign country and not really speaking the language, it was difficult to understand the details. Neither of us had visited the US at that time, so I don't think we fully realized the immense significance of what had happened. The overwhelming grief felt by the locals who explained to us exactly what had happened made it clear, however, that the whole world was in shock.

After that a huge political scandal re-erupted in the UK. Originally making headline news in 1962, major damage was caused to the then current British government of Conservative Prime Minister Harold Macmillan. In the autumn of 1963, it was still big news, and even on the little island of Majorca was still a big topic of conversation. It was known as the Profumo Affair and originated from a sexual liaison between the Secretary of State for War, a man named John Profumo, who was alleged (and later admitted) to having had an affair with an aspiring and unsuccessful young model named Christine Keeler, who, it turned out, was also sleeping with a Soviet agent!

* * * * *

Of all the traumatic events in my lifetime, Tuesday, September 11, 2001, had the greatest effect and certainly changed the world from free-spirited living to fear of death and destruction from terrorism.

Living in California, I remember getting up at the usual time around 7:30 or so, feeding the dog, and making the coffee as I watched my morning breakfast show. Except the morning breakfast show wasn't on. Peter Jennings, anchor of ABC television's World News was there instead and looked grim as he related the beginning of what looked totally unbelievable to me. The events in New York and Washington seemed like an advertisement for some action film as I watched a plane fly into a skyscraper. I wasn't at all sure what was happening except that it looked serious, but I had my routine to follow so off I went on the morning walk. It was only when I returned some thirty minutes later to images of destruction and chaos that I fully realized the devastating extent of the attacks.

A friend and associate living in Manhattan was on her way to a breakfast meeting in the World Trade Center at 9am that morning. As she made her way toward the building, the first plane hit. It was so shocking that it took days before she had any real comprehension of what had happened; she had gone into shock. However, at the time automatic survival instincts kicked in and she just ran from the smoke and falling ash occasionally looking back but more intent on getting as far away as she could. The air was so full of smoke and debris. She said she could hardly breathe, and everyone around her was panic stricken and terrified.

It is said that almost everyone knows someone either directly or indirectly with a friend or relative who lost his or her life in that disaster. My closest association was a friend in the San Diego area with whom I had worked in real estate. Her daughter and son-in-law with their young child had been visiting the Big Apple from Hawaii. After September 11, she never heard from them again.

Everyone lit a candle in memory of those killed, and the following Sunday I had a gathering of neighbors in the garden for a dinner which we called "The End of an Era," which indeed it was.

* * * * *

On Tuesday, August 16, 1977, I was at my desk in Greystone Mansion, when one of the other AFI employees came in and told us Elvis Presley was dead. I think we all went into shock. It was so sudden and he was so young. Of course, we didn't know the background at that time or how worn out he was because of all the drugs involved – to help him sleep, to wake him up, to give him energy, to help him relax – a never ending cycle of uppers and downers had taken their toll.

It was another tragic loss to the world of music, as there certainly would never be another King of Rock and Roll in my lifetime. My apologies to Michael Jackson and Prince fans who may well disagree.

* * * * *

When John Lennon was murdered in New York on December 8, 1980, I was still working for AFI but didn't hear the news until I got home in the evening when it was all over the television. I wrote in my diary how upset I was: "couldn't even eat my dinner." It was my generation, he was 40, and I grew up with the Beatles music. It really affected me.

* * * * *

When the news came through that Princess Diana had died in Paris on August 27, 1997, I remember freezing in the doorway to my bedroom and staring unbelieving at the television screen. I was about to change before attending an event I had organized and didn't know if I should go or stay. The phone began to ring. In the end everything was cancelled, and I think that was one day when virtually the entire population didn't leave their TV set for a single moment.

* * * * *

On March 28, 1979, another trauma occurred at one of the nuclear reactors at Three Mile Island in Pennsylvania. It was heralded as the worst accident in U.S. commercial nuclear power plant history.

It was ironic then that on April 4, less than a week later, I should have gone to a screening of *The China Syndrome.* The film told the story of safety cover-ups at a nuclear power plant! Starring Jack Lemmon and Jane Fonda, Michael Douglas was the producer and James Brooks directed. Obviously, it had been shot long before the recent disaster, but it was uncanny how it mirrored the later events.

* * * * *

And so life goes on, and momentous events occur almost weekly. The most unlikely situations come about when drones collide and driverless cars do not! What's next on the agenda we ask? No one can say for sure except possibly the great prophet Nostradamus who predicted famine and strife for the next 25 years after 2014.

I prefer a more optimistic view with movies abounding, theatres excelling, and sunshine – and stars -- brightening all our lives!

THE END

List of Photographs

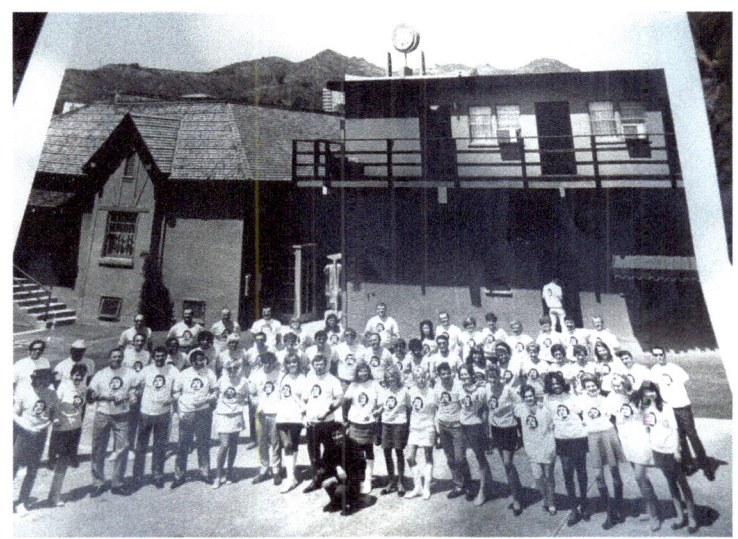

A & M Group Photo with Herb Alpert (kneeling, front center)

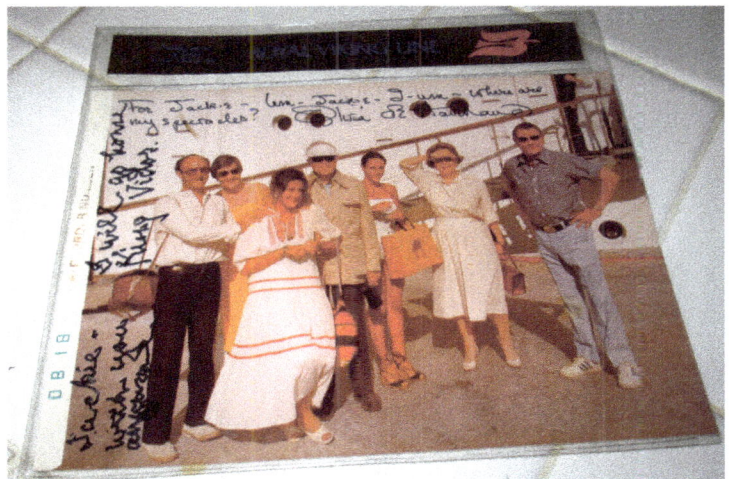

AFI film cruise to Mexico in the early 70's with
Olivia de Havilland, Glen Ford and director, King Vidor.

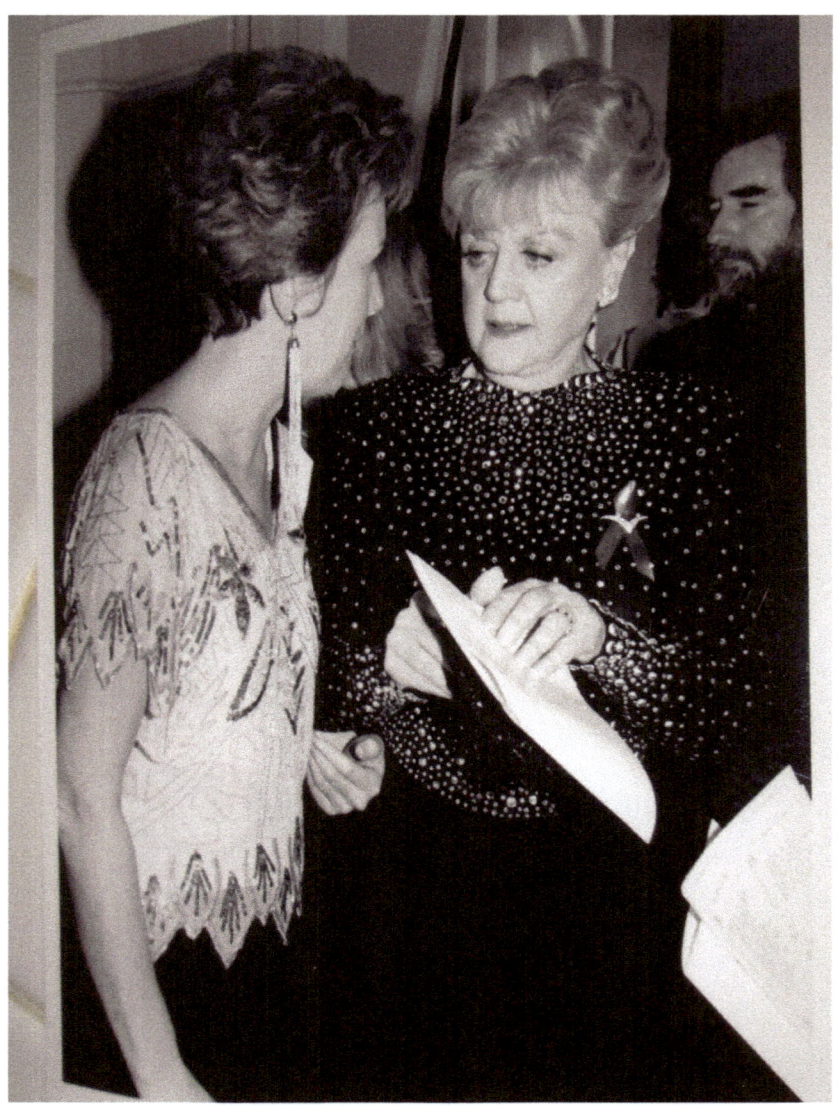

Angela Lansbury checking for her table number at an AFI Dinner.

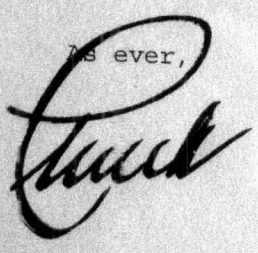

CHARLTON HESTON

October 4, 1999

Dear Jackie:

    I came home from the East Coast to find your letter: I'm sorry you're not going to be with the AFI but delighted to know you're still among us for other projects. I have relied on you enormously for your tender care and professional attention and hope to be able to continue to do so. You're a good person: good things will happen for you.

    I send you my warm best wishes in your new endeavor and look forward to speaking with you often.

As ever,

Chuck

Letter from Charlton Heston.

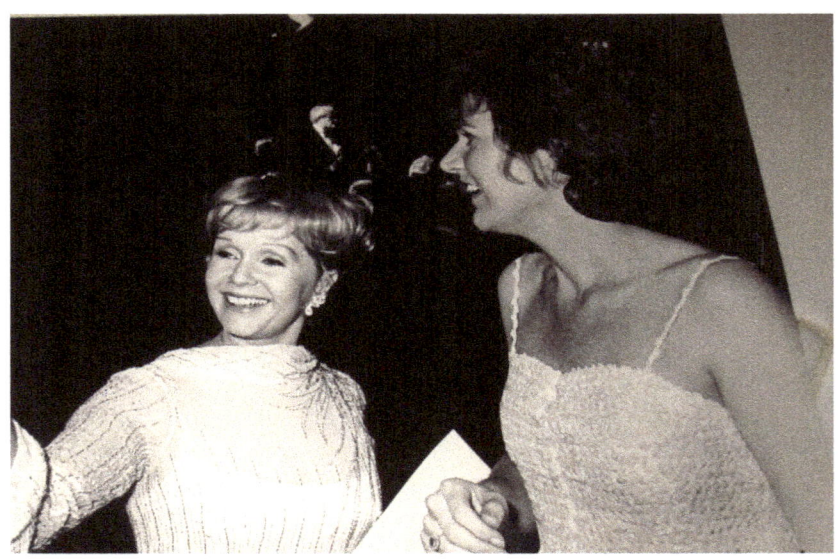

Debbie Reynolds enjoys the festivities at an AFI Dinner.

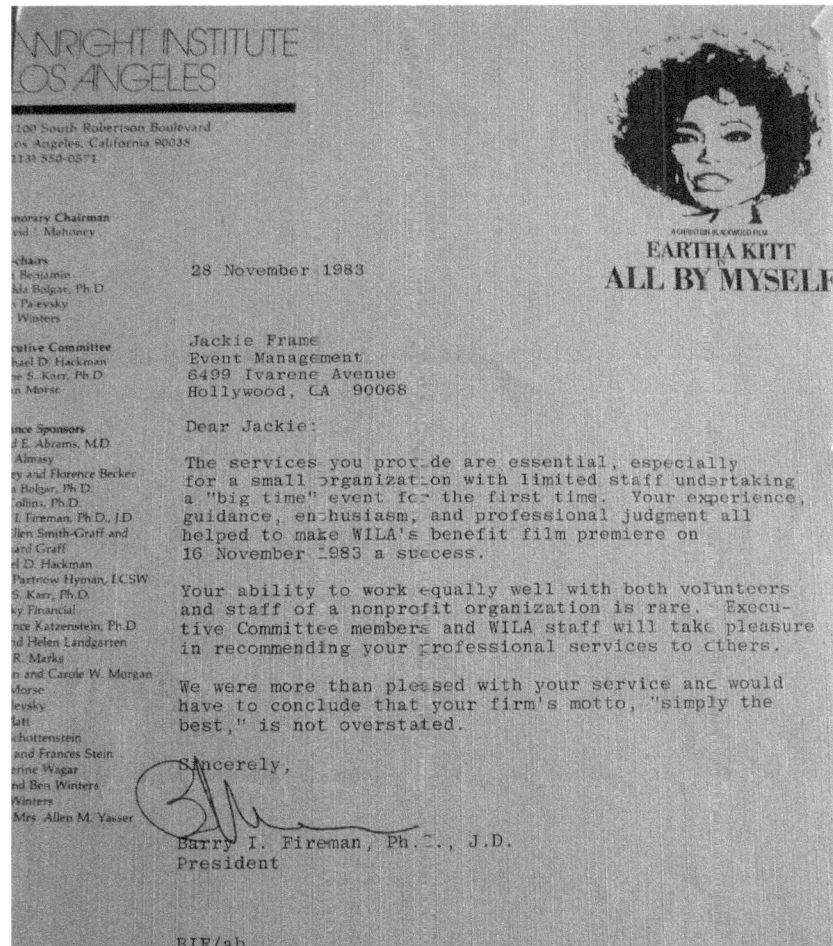

Letter from YPO after screening of Eartha Kitt movie.

FRANK CAPRA
BOX 980
LA QUINTA, CALIFORNIA 92253

May 11, 1982

Jackie Frame
6499 Ivarene Avenue
Hollywood, CA 90068

Dear Jackie:

    I love you, I congratulate you, and I kiss you for the marvelous, marvelous way you ran the AFI award show.

    So many people have said this to me that I thought I would pass it on.

Love,

Frank Capra

Letter from director, Frank Capra.

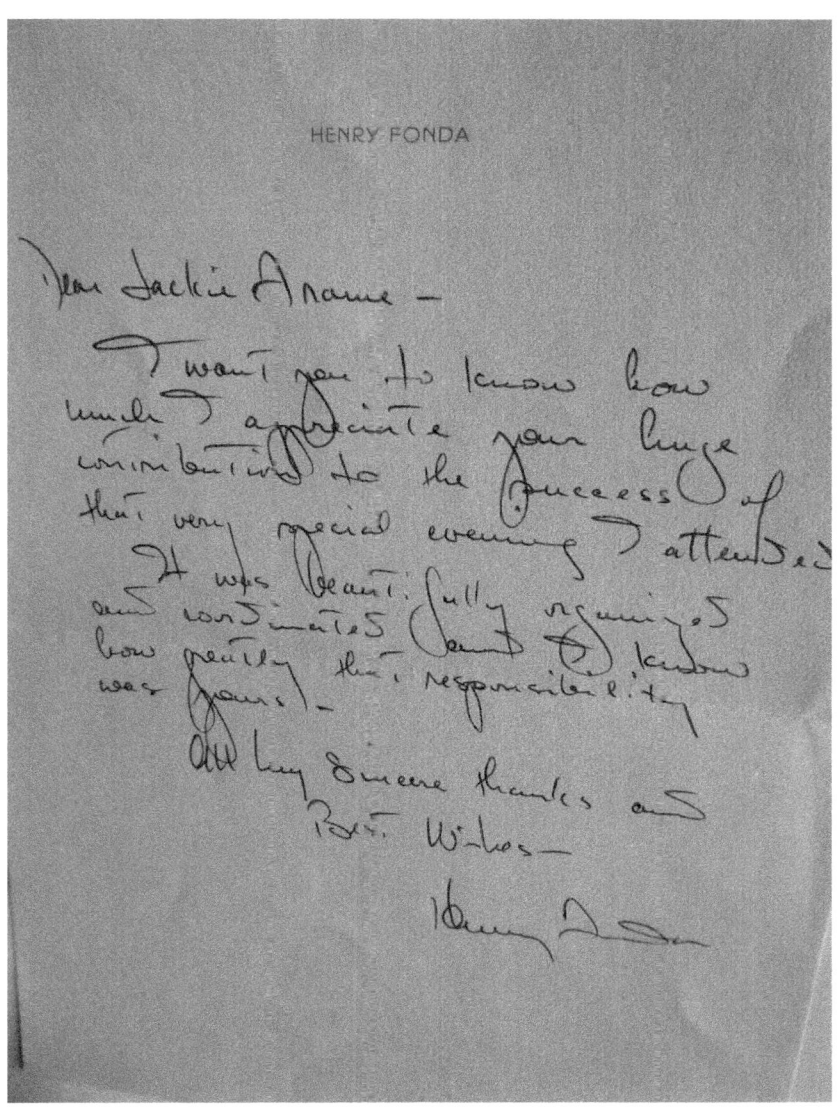

Letter from Henry Fonda.

JACK LEMMON

March 17, 1988

Dear Jackie and Judy,

Just a quickie before I take off for yet another Pro-Am tournament. (I think I get invited to these things purely as comedy relief.)

I just wanted to thank you for the lovely flowers and for all your efforts on behalf of the award dinner.

It was a wonderful evening and you have my undying gratitude.

If you get a chance please thank Ann Wells and Arthur for me -- I'm running out of time before I have to dig divots.

Best always,

Jack

Ms. Jackie Frame & Ms. Judith Mitchell
American Film Institute
2021 North Western Avenue
P. O. Box 27999
Los Angeles, California 90027

Letter from Jack Lemmon.

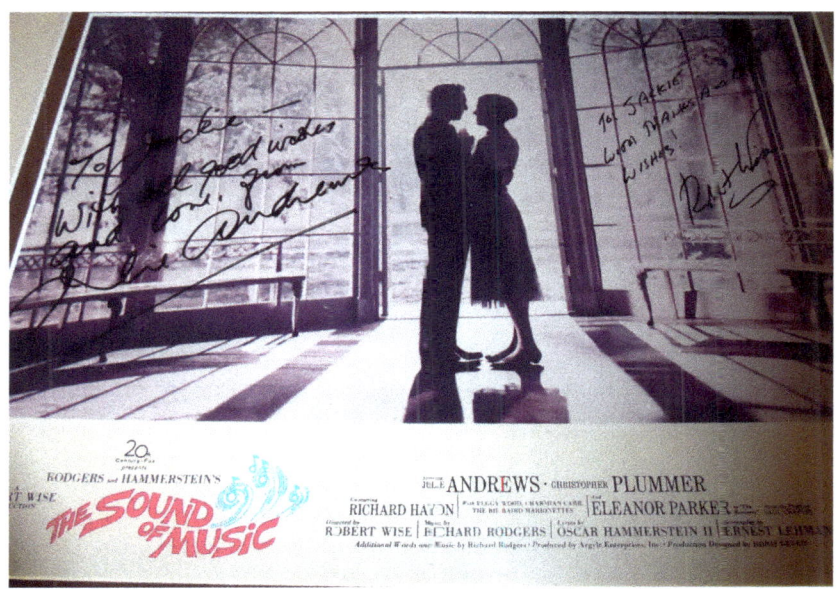

Poster from "The Sound of Music" autographed by Julie Andrews and director, Robert Wise.

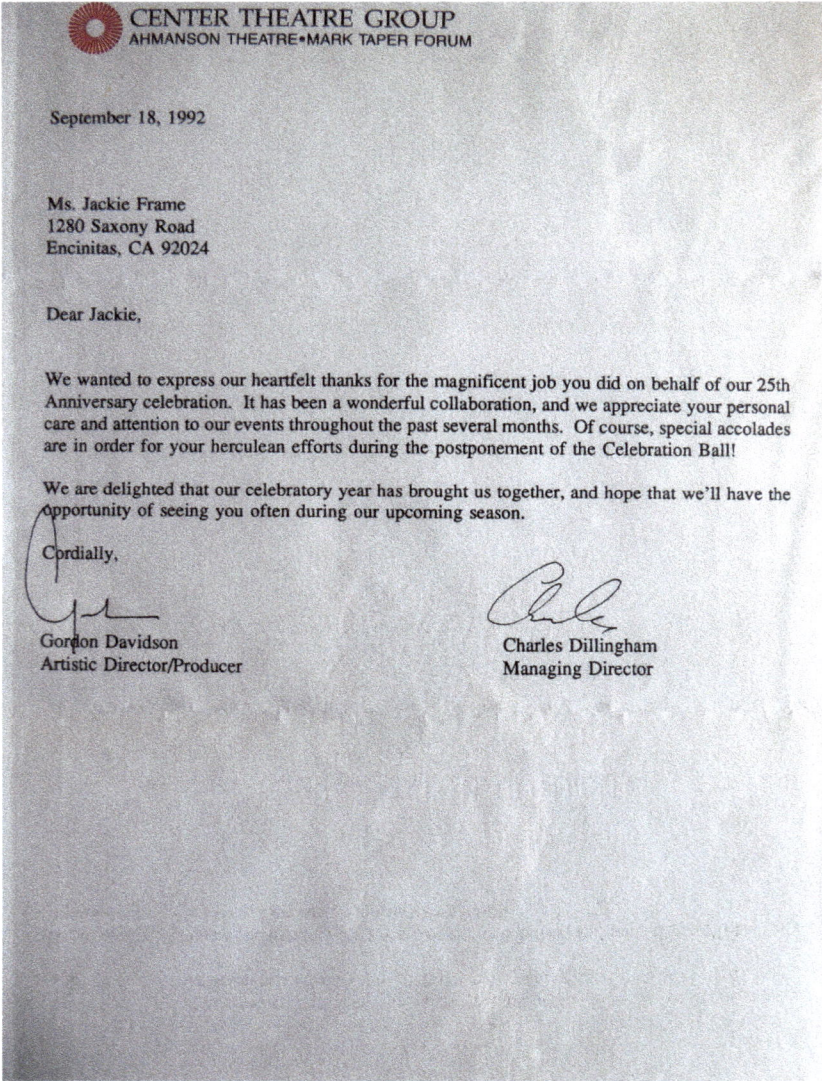

Letter from LA Music Center - Center Theatre Group execs. Gordon Davidson and Charles Dillingham.

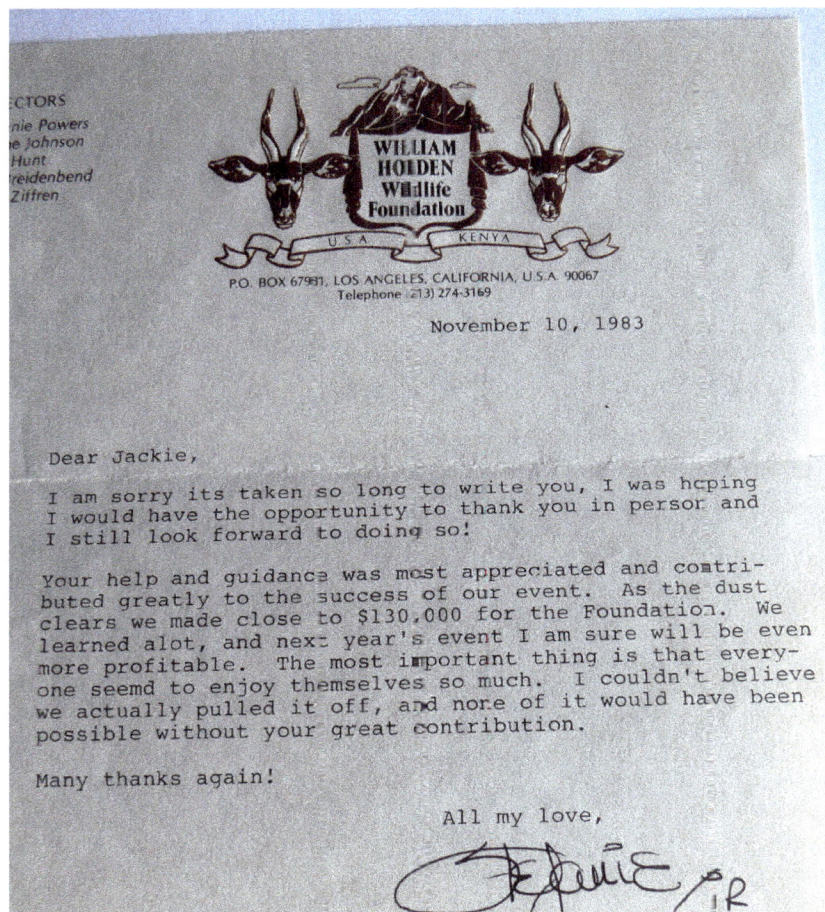

Letter from Stefanie Powers on behalf
of the William Holden Wildlife Foundation.

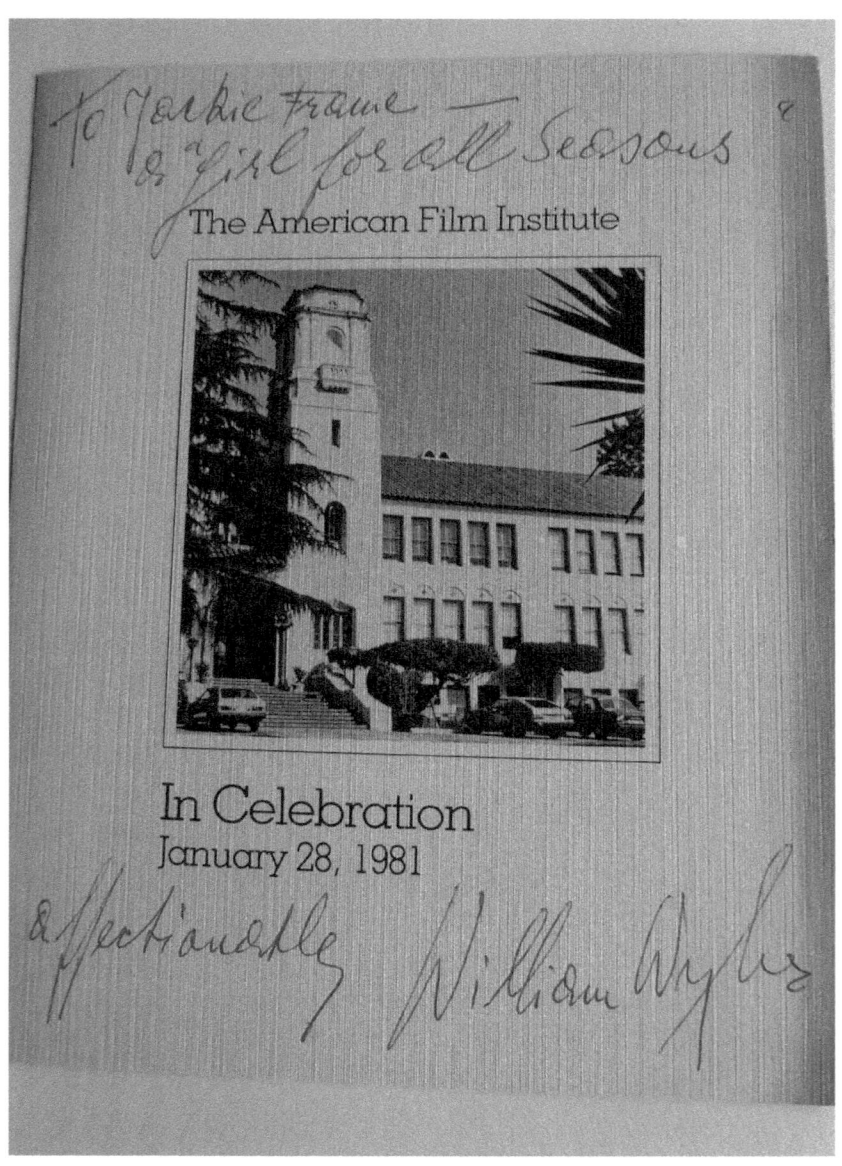

From director, William Wyler.

Index

24 (series) 172
77 Sunset Strip 22
400 Blows, The 51-52

A Little Night Music 200
A&M Records 31, 32-42, 159
Abdul, Paula 89
Academy Awards ("Oscars") 27-28
Academy of Motion Picture Arts and Sciences (AMPAS), 27-28
Adelson, Merv 113, 147
Adjani, Isabelle 47-48
Adventures of Robin Hood, The 21, 172-173
Aga Khan, Princess Yasmin 87
Agassi, Andre 8-9
Agopian, Michael 75
Agutter, Jenny 63
Alda, Alan 70, 90, 140
Alexander, Jane 201
Alfie 2
All About Eve 85
All By Myself 43
All in the Family 113, 192
All the Right Moves 83
Allen, Irwin 59, 122-123, 168, 192, 193
Allen, Sheila 59
Allen, Steve 62, 80, 193
Alley, Kirstie 91
Alpert, Herb 33, 34, 37
Alzheimer's Foundation 87
Amadeus 185
American Comedy Awards 92
American Film Institute, The (AFI) 3, 25, 27, 42, 48, 49, 54, 57, 58-59, 64-67, 73-74, 78, 80, 86, 88, 117-133, 135-155, 157-160, 161, 165-166, 174, 175-176, 177-178, 183, 185, 187, 188, 190, 192, 194-195, 196, 197, 197-198, 206-207, 211-212, 212
Amnesty International 79-81
Amsterdam, Morey 22
Anderson, Judith 124
Anderson, Marian 174
Andrews, Anthony 90, 189-190
Andrews, Dana 26, 167
Andrews, Julie 42-43, 48, 125
Andrews Sisters, The 4
Ann-Margret 89, 197
Annabel's 102
Anne, Princess Royal 102
Applause 185
Archerd, Army 154-155
Arsenic and Old Lace 130
As Time Goes By 199
Astaire, Fred 64-67, 152, 168, 175, 200

Bacall, Lauren 140, 162, 198
Bacharach, Burt, 33, 34-35
Baddeley, Hermione 195
Baez, Joan 33, 41-42
Balanchine, George 175
Ball, Lucille 22, 27
Bancroft, Anne 52, 124
Band Wagon, The 67
Barkin, Ellen 178
Barry, Gene 99
Barrymore, Drew 72
Bart, Lionel 15
Baryshnikov, Mikhail 67, 121
Bassey, Shirley 7
Baxter, Anne 85
Beale, Betty 104
Beatles, The 23-24, 30, 39
Begelman, David 54

Begelman, Gladyce 54
Belles of St. Trinians, The 195
Belmondo, Jean-Paul 51
Belushi, Jim 197
Ben-Hur 26, 121, 127, 166
Bennett, Alan 144
Bennett, Tony 112
Benning, Annette 126
Benny, Jack 67
Benson, Robby 68, 69
Bergen, Candace 126, 178
Bergman, Alan and Marilyn 125, 126
Bergman, Ingrid 49, 124
Bergman, Jerry 83
Berle, Milton 21, 91, 130
Bernstein, Haim 68
Best Years of Our Lives, The 26, 127
Beyond the Fringe 80, 143-144
Bikel, Theodore 126
Bill, Tony 128-129
Birds, The 124
Birth of a Nation, The 27, 158
Bishop, Joey 21, 22, 96, 100
Blakeley, Susan 79
Blazing Saddles 53
Blue Hawaii 55
Blue Skies 65
Bodyguard, The 198
Bogarde, Dirk 92
Bogart, Henry 48, 162
Bolshoi Ballet 93
Bond, Audrey 209-210
Borgnine, Ernest 123, 126, 193-194
Boulting, Roy 137
Bradley, Tom 61, 125
Brando, Marlon 197
Brasil 66 35
Breakfast at Tiffany's 26, 48
Breathless 51
Bricusse, Leslie 31, 48
Brideshead Revisited 189
Bridge on the River Kwai, The 90
Brief Encounter 90
British Broadcasting Corporation (BBC) 14, 15

Broadway Melody of 1940 67
Brocolli, Albert 91, 192
Brooks, James 212-213
Brooks, Mel 52-53, 79, 124
Brosnan, Pierce 63
Broussard, Rebecca 178
Brown, David 112
Brown, Helen Gurley 112
Brynner, Yul 21, 85
Buchwald, Art 67
Burnett, Carol 122
Burns, George 67, 123, 193, 194
Burton, Richard 21, 201
Butch Cassidy and the Sundance Kid 158
Buttons, Red 126, 140, 193

Cabaret 26, 90
Caeser, Sid 62, 91
Caesar's Palace 53
Cagney, James 67
Cahn, Sammy 67, 89
Caine, Sir Michael 1-4, 11, 71, 123, 124, 193
Caine Mutiny Court Martial 166
Call the Midwife 63
Cannel, Stephen 91
Capitol Records 12, 23, 24-25
Capra, Frank 59, 121, 130, 145-145, 187, 192
Carroll, Diahann 112
Carpenters, The (Karen and Richard) 33, 35-36, 37-38
Carr, Charmian 126
Carr, Vikki 11
Carvey, Dana 198
Casablanca 48, 54
Caulfied, Maxwell 137
Champ, The 49
Chaplin, Geraldine 184
Chakiras, George 126
Charisse, Cyd 67, 89
Charles, Prince of Wales 102
Chase, Chevy 125
Chasen, Ronni 91
Chayefsky, Paddy 121-122, 193
Cher 178

Chevalier, Maurice 71
Cheyenne 20
China Syndrome, The 212-213
Chosen, The 67
Clockwork Orange, A 185
Crichton, Michael 124-125
Child, Julia 140, 141
Christie, June 22
Christy, George 59, 129
Churchill, Sir Winston 131
Citizen Kane 50, 125, 175-176
Cleese, Alyce Faye 141
Cleese, John 140, 141-142
Clooney, George 126, 196-197
Clooney, Rosemary 62
Close Encounters of the Third Kind 91
Coburn, James 140
Cocker, Joe 33, 38-40
Cogan, Alma 7
Colbert, Claudette 130, 187
Cole, Nat King 21
Collins, Joan 1
Colman, Ronald 130
Columbo 91
Compton, Lord Spencer 101-103
Connery, Sean 124
Conrad, Jess 15
Cook, Peter 144
Cooke, Alistair 28
Cooke, John 28
Cosmopolitan 112
Cotton, Joseph 124
Count Basie 98
Coward, Noel 137
Crawford, Christina 78
Crawford, Joan 78
Crosby, Bing 4
Cruise, Tom 83, 198
Curtis, Tony 151, 162
Cyrano 63

Daily Variety 154
Damone, Vic 112
Dances With Wolves 198
David, Clive 60-62, 70-71, 103, 106, 109, 110, 114, 147-148

Davis, Bette 48, 85, 145-146, 161, 194-195, 203
Davis, Billy 81
Davis, Clive 60
Davis, Sammy, Jr. 4, 89, 96, 100
Dawber, Pam 91
Day, Doris 128
Days of Wine and Roses, The 25
Dean, James 51, 161, 162
DeLuise, Dom 53, 125
Dench, Dame Judi 198-199
Dene, Terry 15
de Havilland, Olivia 143, 172-175
De Niro, Robert 122
Devane, William 172
DeVito, Danny 198
Densen-Gerbr, Judianne 77
Diamond, Neil 67, 125
Diana, Princess of Wales 103, 212
Dick Van Dyke Show, The 12
Dickinson, Angie 54, 159, 198
Disneyland 2
Doctor Doolittle 48
Donahue, Troy 22
Double Indemnity 129
Douglas, Kirk 90, 139-140, 198
Douglas, Michael 90, 139-140, 161, 212
Downing, Jerry 74
Dr. Zhivago 90
Dreyfus, Richard 112
Driving Miss Daisy 112
Dunaway, Faye 151, 178
Dunne, Irene 124
Dylan, Bob 205
Dynasty 85, 107, 124

Eagles, The 37
Earthquake 165
East of Eden 51
Easter Parade 65
Edwards, Blake 48
Egyptian Theatre 21
Elizabeth, Queen 101
Ennis, Mr. and Mrs. Charles 84
Elephant Man, The 50
Erwin, Bill 81

E.T. The Extra-Terrestrial 72
Evans, Linda 107

Fairbanks, Douglas 21, 187
Faith, Adam 15
Fantasy Island 26
Farr, Felicia 126
Farrow, Mia 48, 95, 124, 161
Ferguson, Sarah, Duchess of York 103
Ferrer, José 62-63
Ferrer, Miguel 62-63
Field of Dreams 198
Fields, Gracie 6
Finch, Peter 122
Finsbury Park Empire 6-7
Fitzgerald, Ella 4
Fitzgerald, Geraldine 194-195
Fletcher, Louise 178
Flying Down to Rio 65
Flynn, Errol 172
Fonda, Amy 139
Fonda, Bridget 139
Fonda, Henry 27, 54, 124, 138-139, 161, 168, 192, 201
Fonda, Jane 138-139, 212
Fonda, Peter 139
Fonda, Shirlee 54, 138
Fontaine, Joan 143
Ford, Betty 64, 66
Ford, Glenn 149-150, 172
Forman, Milos 185
Forsyth, Bruce 5
Forsythe, John 107, 124
Fortensky, Larry 163
Fosse, Bob 67
Four Freshmen, The 2
Franciosa, Tony 99-100
Frankenheimer, John 126
Freeman, Morgan 112
French Connection, The 185
Friedkin, Billy 185
French Chef, The 141
Frost, Sir David 112, 113, 144
Funny Face 67, 200
Furry, Billy 15

Gable, Clark 130, 167, 187
Garland, Judy 4
Gardner, Ava 162
Garner, James 21, 201
Garr, Terri 79
Garson, Greer 61
Gavin, John 128
Gay, Russell 110
General Electric 14
General Hospital 85
Get Smart 52-53
Getty, Ann 112-113
Getty, Gordon 112-113
Ghost and Mrs. Muir, The 53
Giant 163, 188, 189
G.I. Blues 55, 168
Gielgud, Sir John 195-196
Gigi 71
Gingold, Hermione 71
Gish, Lillian 3, 27, 61, 158
Godard, Jean-Luc 51
Godfather, The 122
Going South 168
Grade, Lord Lew 112
Graduate, The 52
Graham, Billy 201-202
Grant, Cary 124, 130, 192
Grauman, Sid 21, 22
Grauman's Theatre 21
Great Escape, The 20
Great Expectations, 90
Greystone Mansion 25, 26, 48-49, 54, 121, 128, 184, 211
Griffin, Merv 62, 88, 126
Griffith, D. W. 27, 158
Guinness, Sir Alec 195
Guinness Book of World Records 5

Haley, Bill, and His Comets 7
Hall, Lani 35
Hamlisch, Marvin 126
Hancock, Tony 6-7
Hancock's Half Hour 6
Hanks, Tom 127
Hardin, Ty 20
Harmon, Mark 91
Harris, David, 41

Harrison, Rex 21, 71
Hart to Hart 92, 161, 170, 171
Harvey 191
Hawn, Goldie 91
Hayes, Helen 191-192
Hayman, D'Arcy 184
Hayworth, Rita 87
HBO 70
Head, Edith 125
Hedren, Tippi 124
Hefner, Hugh 125
Heifetz, Jay 47
Heifetz, Jascha 47
Henley, Don 37, 38
Henreid, Paul 48
Henry VIII 102
Hepburn, Audrey 21, 26, 67, 200
Heston, Chartlon 26, 54-55, 67, 85, 123, 124, 128-129, 157-158, 165-167, 167, 197
Heston, Lydia 54
Hicks, Colin 16
High Anxiety 53
Hill, George Roy 158
Hiller, Arthur 91, 124, 126, 185
Hinkley, David 79
History of the World, Part I 53
Hitchcock, Sir Alfred 123-125, 132
Hoffman, Dustin 52, 135-136
Holden, William 19, 131-132, 161, 170-171
Hollywood Bowl 21, 47
Hollywood Palladium 22, 100
Hollywood Reporter 59, 129
Hope, Bob 4
Hopkins, Anthony 50
Hopkins, Barry 36
Hopper, Hedda 22
Howling, The 71
Hudson, Rock 189
Hugo, Victor 47
Hunter, Tab 22
Huston, Angelica 79, 91
Huston, John 78, 79
Hutton, Betty 63

I Married Dora 62

Immaculate Heart College 128
In the Heat of the Night 158
Innocent, The 48-49
Ipcress File, The 2
Irons, Jeremy 189
Ironside 91
It Happened One Night 130, 187, 188
It's A Wonderful Life 130, 191

Jane Eyre 175
Jarre, Maurice 91
Jaws 112
Jefferson, Thomas 103
Jeffersons, The 113, 192
Jobs, Steve 41, 205
Joffery Ballet, 93-94
Jones, Quincy 33, 125
Julie & Julia 141

Kadar, Jan 185
Kagan, Jeremy 68
Kass, Ron 1-2
Kaye, Danny 4
Keeler, Christine 210
Keller, Helen 52
Kelly, Gene 67, 91
Kelly, Grace 192
Kennedy Center Honors, 100, 174
Kennedy, John F. 162, 172, 208, 210
Kennedy, Robert F. 208
Kent, Linda 164-165
Kentucky Derby 34
Killing Fields, The 80
King, Alan 68
King, Rodney, 206
Kingston Trio, The 21
Kinn, Maurice 15-16
Kissinger, Henry 54
Kitt, Eartha 6, 43-45
Kleiner, Arthur 168
Kluge, Mr. and Mrs. John 103-115
Kojak 91
Kristofferson, Kris 81
Kubrick, Stanley 185

LaBrea Inn 1-2
Laine, Frankie 4
Lancaster, Burt 21
Landau, Edie 68, 69
Landau, Ely 68, 69
Lange, Hope 53
Lange, Jessica 121
Lange, Kelly 63
Lansbury, Angela 120-121
Lasker, Jay 23-24
Laugh In 92
Laura 167
Lawford, Peter 96, 100
Lawrence, Carol 62
Lawrence of Arabia, 89-90, 91
Lazarus, James 81-82
Lean, Sir David 86, 89, 90, 137
Lear, Mr. and Mrs. Norman 113, 192
Lee, Peggy 22
Leigh, Janet 124
Leigh, Vivien 137, 142-143
Leighton, Margaret 195
Lemmon, Jack 25, 90, 91, 126, 129, 151-153, 190, 212
Lennon, John 212
Leon, Jean 162
Lewis, Jerry 5-6
Lewis, Judy 167, 170
Liberace 62
Liberty Records 1, 32, 95
Lies My Father Told Me 185
Little, Rich 91, 92, 125
Little House on the Prairie 195
Little Romance, A 142
Livingston, Alan 132
London Philharmonic 47
Longet, Claudine 35
Lost Horizon 130
Lost Weekend, The 129
Love Story 91, 185
Love With The Proper Stranger 20
Lucas, George 127
Lynch, David 198

MacArthur 168
MacGraw, Ali 91

MacLaine, Shirley 61, 89, 96, 99, 101, 129, 140, 151, 178
MacLauchlan, Janet 99
Magnificent Ambersons, The 85
Malden, Karl 26, 126, 193, 198
Maltese Falcon, The 78
Mamoulian, Rouben 185
Man Who Knew Too Much, The 191
Man Who Shot Liberty Valance, The 191
Manchester, Melissa 126
Mancini, Henry 21, 22
Mann's Chinese Theatre 22
Mansfield, Jayne 162
Manulis, Martin 25, 157, 188, 196
Marquee Club 16
Marsh, Jean 161
Martin, Dean 5, 21, 22, 96, 100
Martin, Lloyd 74-75
Martin, Millicent 144
Martin, Pamela Sue 85
Martin, Steve 91
Marty 193
Marx, Groucho 162
Mary, Queen of Scots 102
Mary Tyler Moore Show 158
M*A*S*H 70, 90
Matthau, Walter 79, 91, 151, 152-153, 197
Maude 113, 192, 195
Mayer, Louis B. 27
McBroom, Amanda 80
McCartney, Paul 25
McDowell, Malcolm 80
McDowell, Roddy 189
McGoohan, Patrick 20
McGuire Sisters, The 21
McQueen, Steve 20, 22
Meadows, Jayne 193
Mendes, Sergio 35
Midler, Bette 81
Midnight Lace 128
Miller, Ann 89
Miller, Jonathan 144
Mills, Hayley 137
Mills, Sir John 137

Mills, Juliet 48, 137
Minnelli, Liza 4, 33, 89
Miracle Worker, The 52
Mirisch, Walter 158, 192
Missiles of October, The 172
Mitchell, Guy 16
Monkees, The 126
Monro, Matt 29-30
Montalban, Ricardo 26
Moore, Dudley 80, 130, 143-144
Moore, Mary Tyler 12
Moore, Roger 71
Moreno, Rita 126
Mork and Mindy 91
Morris Angel & Sons 15
Moss, Jerry 33, 34, 39-40, 159
Mr. Smith Goes To Washington 191
Mrs. Miniver 127
Muppet Movie, The 37
Murder She Wrote 121
Mutiny on the Bounty 50
My Fair Lady 21, 71
Myra Breckenridge 121

Name of the Game, The 99, 101
Nanny and the Professor 48
National Health Service (UK) 40
National Register of Historic Places 87
Navon, Benjamin 69
NCIS 91
Neal, Patricia 126, 198
Nesmith, Michael 126
Network 121
New Musical Express 16
Newley, Anthony 31-32, 91
Newman, Paul 112, 142, 162
Nicholas Brothers, The 89
Nicholson, Jack 168, 176-179
Nimoy, Leonard 126
Ninotchka 129
Niven, David 67
Nixon, Richard 103, 112
No Man's Land 195-196
Now, Voyager 48
Nutcracker, The 94

Odyssey House 77
Oliver 15
Oliver Twist 90
Olivier, Lawrence, 142-143
Olson, Nancy (Livingston) 131, 162, 205-206
Onassis, Aristotle 103
O'Neal, Ryan 91
Osmond Brothers, The 22
O'Toole, Peter 90
Owens, Gary 122

Palladium, The (London) 5, 6
Pan, Hermes 67
Parent Trap, The 137
Parents Anonymous 86-87
Patton 185
Paul Sills' Story Theatre 47
Pawnbroker, The 2
Peck, Gregory 21, 27, 54, 61, 126, 140, 142, 157, 158-159, 159-160, 161, 168
Peck, Veronique 54, 159-160
Pell, George 95
Pena, Elizabeth 62
Peppard, George 26
Perkins, Anthony 124
Perlman, Rhea 198
Peters, Bernadette 67
Petrie, Dan 126
Peyton Place, 48
Philadelphia Story, The 191
Philbin, Regis 122
Philomena 199
Pink Panther 48
Pinter, Harold 92, 195-196
Pitt, Brad 202-203
Place in the Sun, A 138
Playboy 125
Plummer, Christopher 125, 200-201
Pocketful of Miracles 145
Poitier, Sydney 206
Polyanna 137
Poseidon Adventure, The 92, 168-169
Powell, Eleanor 67

Powell, Julie 141
Powers, Stefanie 92, 161, 170-172
Preminger, Otto 167
Presley, Elvis 54-55, 101, 168, 211-212
Preston, Billy 39
Previn, Dory 67
Pride and Prejudice 199
Procol, Harum 33
Producers, The 53
Profumo, John 210
Prowse, Juliet 89
Puck, Wolfgang 171

Queen's Theatre 31
Quinn, Anthony 154
Quinn, Yolanda 154

Railway Children, The 63
Ramsay, Lord and Lady 113
Ray, Johnny 4
Razor's Edge, The 85
Rear Window 191
Rebecca 124, 142-143
Rebel Without A Cause 51, 161
Reddy, Helen 36, 125
Redford, Robert 112
Redgrave, Corin 135
Redgrave, Jemma 135
Redgrave, Lynn 135-136
Redgrave, Sir Michael 135
Redgrave, Vanessa 32, 135, 136
Reiner, Carl 53
Remick, Lee 25
Rich, Dareth 31
Rich Man, Poor Man 79
Richard, Cliff 7, 8-9, 36-37
Richardson, Joely 135
Richardson, Natasha 135
Richardson, Sir Ralph 195-196
Rickles, Don 140
Riddle, Nelson 96
Riklis, Meshulam 68, 69
Rivers, Johnny 20
Robin Hood: Men in Tights 53
Rockefeller, Nelson 77
Rockford Files, The 91, 201

Rodgers, Richard 175
Rogers, Ginger 67
Rolling Stone 39
Rolling Stones, The 16, 126
Roman Holiday 160
Romeo and Juliet 185
Rosemary's Baby 48
Roxy, The 49
Rubinstein, Arthur 175
Rumford Fair Housing Act 21
RWB Productions 74
Ryan, Pat 60
Ryan's Daughter 90, 137

Salvation Army 178-179
Samms, Emma 85
Samuel Goldwyn Theater 28
Samuelson, Peter 85
Sand, Paul 47
Sanford and Son 192
Saturday Night Live 144
Schaffner, Franklin J. 124, 126, 185
Scheider, Roy 112
Schell, Maximilian 67
Schickele, Peter (P.D.Q. Bach) 47
Schlatter, George 92
Schlesinger, John 52
Schneider, Jack 59
Scorsese, Martin 129
Screaming Lord Sutch 16
Seberg, Jean 51
Secret Agent 20
Sedaka, Neil 126
Seinfeld 81
Selleck, Tom 80, 126
Servant, The 92
Sevalas, Telly 91
Shadows, The 7
Shakespeare in Love 199
Shall We Dance? 65
Shatner, William 124, 126
Shearing, George 22
Sheinberg, Sid 127
Shell Oil 14
Shenandoah 191
Shore, Dinah 22

Silence of the Lambs 50
Silk Stockings 67
Sills, Beverly 112
Simmons, Jean 198
Sinatra, Frank 4, 21, 22, 61, 95-99, 100, 103, 176, 200
Sirens of the Sea 167
Smilin' Through 22
Smith, Dame Maggie 143
Sojourn House, 70
Some Like It Hot 91, 129
Sound of Music, The 42, 50, 125, 126, 200
Spaceballs 53
Spielberg, Steven 72, 124, 127, 151
Springfield, Rick 49
Springsteen, Bruce 125
Stack, Robert 99, 183-185
Stallone, Sylvester 198
Stanfill, Terry 192
Stanwyck, Barbara 64, 139, 197
Star is Born, A 36
Star Wars 127
Starlight Foundation 85
Steele, Tommy 16-17
Steenburgen, Mary 80, 178
Steiger, Rod 2, 67, 69
Stern, Stewart 51
Stevens, Cat 33
Stevens, George 49, 188, 189
Stevens, George, Jr. 118, 152, 157-158, 160, 163, 174, 188
Stewart, James 57, 124, 130, 160, 191-193
Sting, The 112, 158
Stone, Christopher 71-72
Story of Adele H. 47
Straight, Beatrice 79
Streep, Meryl 79
Streets of San Francisco, The 26
Streisand, Barbara 36, 67, 125
Sunday Bloody Sunday 52
Sunday Night at the Palladium 5
Sunset Boulevard 19, 129, 131-132, 162, 205
Sunshine, Morton 70
Sunshine Boys, The 194

Swanson, Gloria 131-132
Swing Time 65

Talmadge, Norma 22
Tandy, Jessica 112
Tango 49
Taylor, Elizabeth 21, 113, 163-165
Tea With Mussolini 199
Ten Commandments, The 85
Terrail, Patrick 171
That Was The Week That Was 112, 144
This Is Your Life 15
Thomas, Danny 22
Three Sisters 143
Tillis, Mel 113-114
To Kill A Mockingbird 158
Todd, Mary 167
Top Hat 65
Travolta, John 197
Truffaut, François 47, 51-52, 124
Tucker, Sophie 4
Turner, Ike 101
Turner, Kathleen 178
Turner, Tina 101
Twin Peaks 198

Valentine, Trevor 71
Vallee, Rudy 63
Van Dyke, Dick 21
Variety Clubs International 70
Vee Jay Records 23-24
Vertigo 191
Vidor, King 49, 172
Visconti, Luchino 48
von Damm, Helen 113

Wagner, Robert 27, 140, 143, 161, 161-162, 170, 172, 197
Walker, Clint 20
Wallace, Dee 71-72
Wallis, Hal 54-55
Walters, Barbara 113, 146-149
Wambaugh, Joseph 191
War and Peace 49
Warner, John 113, 145
Warwick, Dionne 62

Washbourne, Mona 191
Wasserman, Lew 127
Webb, Michael 168
Welles, Orson 43, 50, 85, 175-176
West, Mae 201-202
West Side Story 50, 126
West Wing, The 172
What's My Line 15
Whistle Down the Wind 137
Who Stole My Childhood 74, 86
Why We Fight (series) 131
Whitcomb, Ian 191
Widmark, Richard 79
Wilde, Marty 15
Wilder, Billy 91, 129-130, 159
Wilder, Gene 124
Williams, Andy 21, 22, 35
Williams, Paul 33, 35
Williams, Robin 125
Willie Wonka & The Chocolate Factory 48
Wilson, Nancy 21
Winkler, Henry 140, 197
Winters, Shelley 92
Wise, Millicent 126
Wise, Robert 42, 50, 124, 125-126, 200
Wood, Natalie 20, 21, 27, 61, 143, 161-163
Woodstock 39, 41
Woodward, Joanne 142, 162
Wright Institute 44-45
Wuthering Heights 143, 195
Wyatt, Jane 130
Wyeth, Andrew 49
Wyler, Tilly 127-128
Wyler, William 64, 124, 127-129, 143, 177, 192, 195
Wyman, Jane 124

Yanks 52
Young Frankenstein 53, 79
Young, Loretta 167, 169-170
Young Presidents Organization (YPO) 81-84
Young Winston 50
York, Michael 26, 71, 90, 179, 183

Zadora, Pia 69
Zeffirelli, Franco 185
Zimbalist, Efrem, Jr. 22
Zsigmond, Vilmos 91

www.ingramcontent.com/pod-product-compliance
Lightning Source LLC
Chambersburg PA
CBHW040516220526
45473CB00012B/2880